Claim Your Light

Gaining Insight For A Fulfilling Life

Wayne Benenson, Ph.D
Barb Hughson, Ed.D

Claim Your Light – Gaining Insight for a Fulfilling Life

© Copyright 2017, Wayne Benenson and Barb Hughson

All rights reserved.

IBN: 978-0-9985656-1-3

No part of this book may be reproduced, stored in a retrieval system, or transmitted in any form or by any means, electronic, mechanical, photocopying, recording, or by any information retrieval system, or otherwise without the prior express written consent of the authors, except for the inclusion of brief quotations in critical articles or a review.

Table of Contents

Forward ii

Preface 6

Chapter 1 – Introduction 11

Chapter 2 – Home Plate: Identifying Our Needs 28

Chapter 3 – First Base: Empathy 44

Chapter 4 – Second Base: Grit 64

Chapter 5 – Third Base: Growth Mindset 80

Chapter 6 – Getting to Home Plate: Living With
    Our Questions 101

Author Biography 123

Acknowledgements

This is a book about staying awake despite the temptations all around me to be lulled back to sleep. My deepest thanks go to my students, past and present. They are my true mentors, and have kept me on my toes, creating so many opportunities for learnable moments. This book is also about showing up, every day, with the freshest version of myself. My bottomless thanks go to all those people who believed in me, even when I enthusiastically embraced half-baked ideas, especially Renae, my wife and chief instigator.

Wayne Benenson

When I began my dissertation journey many years ago, I had no idea that the ideas I researched would turn into this book. Again and I again, I learned the lesson of following my instincts and not letting feelings of insecurity hold me back. Thank you, thank you to my family and friends who supported me through the challenges and joys of my doctoral journey. Special thanks go to the members of my dissertation committee who believed in me even when I didn't. They modeled greatness for me!

Barb Hughson

Forward

Books on change, both of personal transformative change and systems change, often overpromise and under-deliver. Why? It's all quite understandable, really, when one equates the expected change as "better" rather than simply "different." Transformation can sound so enticing if a perception of one's identity, life skills or habits leave much to be desired. Who wouldn't want a radical makeover that replaces mindless suffering with a tonic that magically undoes past conditioning? That's the key, isn't it, serving up a potent tonic to blast past a life on automatic pilot? Happily, Wayne and Barb do not offer up the latest elixir to take away the sting of change. They hold up the notion of curiosity to get to the other shore. The process they describe is not new. It is grounded in ancient wisdom that allows us to move forward with new eyes and fresh resolve.

I was impressed by how they moved the conversation of change from surviving life's slings and arrows to actually thriving, from turning adversity into opportunities. How does that work? The short answer is by building capacity. As one increases in their ability to respond to frightful change from a place of vision and compassion rather than ego or self-interest, one's life can be filled with more meaning and contentment. From their educator's perspective, the main question on transformative change boils down to this image:

"What if the person standing in the wings, ready to burst on to the stage in a more vibrant way, was simply waiting for his or her cue?" The main point, for me, is the rock-solid sensibility that every person already has all that he or she needs to live a more vibrant life. One moves from surviving to thriving by knowing yourself at your core and being guided by your inner wisdom. The section on consciousness change as well as the exercises and questions throughout the book allows a new wisdom to bubble up, a new presence to emerge that is integrated, creative and aligned with one's higher purpose.

Ultimately, the way of seeing and thinking and reflecting upon ourselves and environment asks basic questions about a sustainable relationship with the whole web of life. The last chapter is a fine summary of the general process of self-questioning that gives insight to the more specific questions throughout the book. I especially responded to the I-Thou reference at the beginning of the chapter for it reminds the reader the purpose of a re-examined life is to enter into communion with one's fellow human beings. Buber's I-Thou, I-It, philosophy does that; it takes us out of our own little world to engage with our struggling sisters and brothers around us. I also liked the emphasis on the Key 3: empathy, grit and grow mindset. Empathy puts us in touch with the humanity in others and in ourselves. Grit means having the courage to listen to what's going on in the conflict between our inner self and the outer world. Grit backs up one's good intentions. Dostoevski said celebrating love in one's imagination is easy; but loving in one's daily life can be gut wrenching. It's a whole different ball game, to use the analogy in the book, of rounding third and heading for home. Loving in our daily life, both the personal and the public, <u>and</u> caring about sisters and brothers all over this land, is the last great dash for home hoping to arrive safely ahead of the throw coming in from outfield. That throw is, of course, the negativity of one's lesser, fearful self that is used to keep one's true self from reaching home plate. Isn't this how we wake people up to the real game of life? If we do those first two well – empathy and grit, my experience tells me that growth mindset will follow along. First we act, embrace the search for personal transformation, then our view of the world changes to help reinforce the new direction allowing each of us to be the person we were meant to be.

Finally, I was intrigued by the blending of academic explanations with literary and cultural examples as well as pop culture gems to appeal to a wide audience. Mick Jagger and Tagore do indeed address common issues of what human life is all about. I also enjoyed the stories Wayne and Barb shared at the end of each chapter for a personal account of self-actualization. By sharing what may be embarrassing or vulnerable they effectively distance themselves from the overly simple, "me-based" popular works on change which can encourage a siloed selfishness. These authors are believable and trustworthy and accessible. They mix their reactions to the Key 3 – of empathy, grit and growth mindset – with the scholarship of transformative education with a healthy dab of similar perceptions like Buddhist mindfulness and Maslow's hierarchy of needs. This book will, no doubt, appeal to a broad, basically humanistic, audience. *Claim Your Light* is something anyone can do, humanist or religious (or spiritual), and will draw people who are living half-fulfilled lives, of what Thoreau called "lives of quiet desperation," into new possibilities of personal and professional growth. Wayne's and Barb's final sharing puts the reader in touch with two real people who've had their own transformation – personally and professionally – that they want to share with others. It's a sharing most definitely worth your time and attention.

John Corry
Theologian and author
Albuquerque, New Mexico
January 2017

Preface

When I (WB) was a teenager I couldn't get enough of the Beach Boys hit "Good Vibrations." It played constantly in my head. Interestingly enough, it still does today. I am attracted to both the beat ("Good, good, good . . . good vibrations") and the message. Back then, the notion that I had the power to change my vibe was a new thought for me. Imagine that . . . I could recalibrate my mood, like flipping the channels on the radio dial, whenever my equilibrium had been disturbed. I could alter my attitude when my mood soured. I could get unstuck after a disappointment or setback. Nevertheless, I wondered how and where I could find those good vibrations. This book is about finding your vibration, your most authentic self.

Part of that treasure hunt is recognizing the seeds of your own authenticity. The signs are everywhere but intensely personal: a dream that keeps coming back, a song lyric that plays on a continuous loop in your head, a snippet of an overheard conversation that feels like it was meant just for you. It's fair to ask if these random-but-important connections represent a pipeline to the deepest parts of your soul or are simply pipedreams of ephemeral desires. A quick and dirty way to get the goods is to ask this simple question: does the sign astonish you? That energy, pulsating from your roots – your vibration – holds the blueprint of your spiritual

DNA. Standing in your own light means reconnecting with your most primal sense of self despite the distractions of the day.

However, the ride to what's genuine and great in your life is often bumpy. Those daily distractions represent both dangers and opportunities on your journey to a more vibrant you. Beware of the potholes! The credibility of your most essential self is often exposed in places where there is a lot of friction. Conflict occurs where change is taking place, where your longings rub against your security. How much of that conflict is self-imposed by expectations of perfection? Many folks, including the authors of this book, confuse happiness and perfectionism. For example, an inflated sense of order and appropriateness plays havoc with my personal life. It's as if I have a constant need to prove myself to the world. This creates unnecessary stress, a tendency to micromanage and stifles creativity and flexibility. My cherished notions of perfectionism are hard to sustain and consume time and energy that leads to diminishing returns. Perversely, my dissatisfaction causes me to look for more ways to be "perfect" and I become busier and busier, which just feeds this vicious cycle.

When I stand in my own light I give myself permission to get off the merry-go-round and sample other rides in the amusement park. Perfectionism is usually driven by chronic dissatisfaction, and it is sometimes disguised as self-improvement. There is nothing wrong with improving myself and doing my best, but if the obsession for perfectionism comes from insecurity or fear of being not good enough, then I will never be satisfied no matter how wonderful and perfect everything is. This book can help you make a shift. Can you imagine growing in a new way? Standing in your own light means taking personal responsibility for the experiences in your life. Being accountable to yourself, both who you perceive yourself to be and who you are becoming, means choosing a "both/and" perspective. You hold, with grace and tenderness, <u>both</u> the unwanted habit <u>and</u> the new norm which is coming into being. For example, if your past is littered with failed attempts at managing your finances, then your new behavior is to <u>both</u> acknowledge the unproductive habit, say impulse buying, <u>and</u> embrace the new habit of building up the savings account to afford a big-ticket item.

The craft of becoming a more vibrant person can happen at either end of a continuum. At one pole your focus is on getting unstuck from negativity. Whatever your self-improvement project – losing weight, managing money without fear, or attracting joy and compassion in intimate relationships – you won't be successful until you change your thinking and move your habits of mind from "I can't" to "I can." This book offers a program of three keys – empathy, grit and growth mindset – to help you make that shift. At the opposite end of the spectrum your emphasis is on dissolving the barriers to your calling. This involves consciously deciding what is most truthful for you. Choosing to follow your light will no doubt bring on more heat as you distance yourself from your familiar comfort zone. As the songwriter Don Henley described it: "sometimes you get the best light from a burning bridge." This book offers a recurring refrain of "Listening to Your Inner Quiet" to deepen and nurture your shift in consciousness. As you reimagine the expanded version of yourself, think of these concepts and practices as process knowledge in your psychic toolkit which will increase your confidence in taking on long-avoided challenges.

This transformation of attitudes and actions does not happen in a void. As you become the change you are seeking it is crucial to celebrate your progress. Making a public declaration of your updated changes is a rite of passage as you leave one frame of mind and enter another. It involves a significant change of status in society. Think baptisms or bar mitzvahs, military service or a marriage. Anthropologists have noted three phases to a rite of passage: separation, liminality, and incorporation. In the first phase, people withdraw from their current status and prepare to move from one place or status to another. The second phase is a transition between states, during which one has left one place but has not yet entered or joined the next. Everything seems ambiguous during this period. In the third phase a person has completed the rite of passage and assumed their "new" identity. One re-enters (or reincorporates in) society with one's new status through elaborate rituals and ceremonies, like debutant balls and college graduation. Our culture tends to emphasize ceremony more than ritual. Typically, the missing piece is the societal recognition and reincorporation phase. These initiation rites are fundamental to human growth and development. Please use *Claim Your Light* as a workbook that ultimately marks your transition to your different status, both to the community and to the world of spirit.

Although this book can be used as a stand-alone guide to improvement we have intended for it to support a specific program. The ideas in this book are necessary but insufficient to allow new habits to develop strong roots. We envision planting the tools of transformational change through a combination of live coaching sessions and a 10 week online training. The package of the book (and workbook), the coaching sessions and the online curriculum does two things. First, it offers the most relevant content on how the transformational process works through research-supported learning theory. Second, it offers application examples of successful practice. Along with consciousness-raising activities help individuals or groups will have a roadmap to increase their human capacity. The tagline of our program is this: Gaining insight to solve personal and social problems. If you are committed to the package (books, coaching sessions and online curriculum), we guarantee that insight.

It is our hope that you find value and vitality in this book. May your conscious choice to fully embrace your vibrancy lessen your grasp and increase your reach. We honor your courage to do the work that allows you to shine. As you commit to the journey hold close to your heart these words from Rabindraneth Tagore: "Faith is the bird that feels the light when dawn is still dark."

Wayne Benenson
Barb Hughson
January 2017

Chapter 1

Introduction: Outer Wholeness + Inner Quiet = Hidden Vitality

Can you imagine growing into the person you were meant to be? Hmm, what an audacious question. There's so much to unpack in that provocative question. What does "meant to be" mean? According to whom? And, what nurtures that growth? Who has those magic seeds so I can have my Jack-in-the-beanstalk moment? Okay, okay, perhaps a scaled back question might be: *Can you imagine living your life in a more vibrant way?* Whoa, whoa, wait a minute. My life is already way too complicated and who has time for a social or psychological makeover? All right, all right, let's try one last stab at hooking the golden ring. *What if, hypothetically speaking, the "you" that was meant to be was already amongst us?* What if that person standing in the wings, ready to burst on to the stage in a more vibrant way, was simply waiting for his or her cue? This anticipated metamorphous is similar to Michelangelo's explanation on creating the iconic sculpture of David: "he was already inside the marble, waiting to get out; I just chipped away the outside stone." This book is an instruction manual to chip away the stone to allow your amazing self to appear, unadorned. It's a teacher's guide for learning the process skills to help you construct a new paradigm or worldview. This process knowledge can expand your psychic toolkit and increase your confidence in taking on long-avoided personal challenges.

But wait, you say, not another self-help book! Self-improvement products and services represents a $10 billion per year industry in the US alone. The formula is simple and seductive: just follow these ten easy steps and you will (fill in the blank . . . improve your health . . . lose weight . . . make a fortune, find your sweet heart . . . improve your relationships, etc.) in only ___ short weeks. Don't miss this great opportunity. This pitch works so effectively because it taps into our personal sense of inadequacy in fulfilling the newest version of the American Dream. If only I was a few pounds lighter or a few bucks richer I would be happy, truly happy. Indeed, the lure of a better life is universal, however a quick fix often ends in headaches or heart ache. Why? Two answers provide a partial explanation. The first answer comes from an unproductive sense of time. If we are living – consciously or unconsciously – with a life story from our past or expectations of fulfillment from the future. Sadly, we've given away our personal power. The past is gone, the future is yet to come. We only have control in this present moment. However, as all of the broken promises attest, it's not so easy to stay focused on the now. The second answer comes from an incomplete sense of self. It's the perfection myth eroding our tattered image. If only I was more disciplined, a better planner, less fearful in the face of adversity . . . and on and on and on. Perfect is an awfully high bar for us mortals to strive for, let alone reach. What to do? What to do? Wouldn't it be a relief to know how much weight to put on the footfall of your new path instead of stumbling over the next step? The premise of this book is to take the burden off your shoulders and spread the wealth of making important changes in your life *while in community.* That means reframing the perception of yourself with everyone watching. No doubt your first thought might be: Horrors! No way. How embarrassing. I couldn't possibly do *that*. And that's the whole point. You get to your new "me" by embracing a new "we." By choosing the community which supports our change we tap into a vast reserve of potential power to remake our image of what's possible.

Aaah, but there's more. These two explanations – focusing on the present and sharing my transformation within community – still don't get to the deeper truth of why change is so vexing. What, then, is this deeper truth? The short answer involves allowing ourselves to be more bold in living our purpose and passion. If we want the changes we are seeking to stick, we must be willing to investigate new horizons in our life for our best self to show up. We go broader through practicing what we truly love. In this context, practice means doing what you love over and over again, not begrudgingly but enthusiastically. In *Outliers: The Story of Success,* Malcolm Gladwell repeatedly comments on the "10,000-Hour Rule", claiming that the key to achieving world class expertise in any skill, is, to a large extent, a matter of practicing the correct way, for a total of around 10,000 hours. So, the key to success is changing behavioral patterns by joyfully practicing a new way of responding to our challenges for a long, long time. Nope.

That's necessary but not sufficient. That's still not enough to get you to the finish line.

To get there we must also be willing to also go deeper, to build a new home which allows our soul to shine. Not only must we get excited about our new way of being and learning everything we can about it, we must journey to our underworld where our intuition and imagination and inspiration reside. In that netherworld of fleeting fears and unresolved conflicts from past mistakes we need to reframe who we say we are. (A note of caution: we can get more mileage out of this process if we describe rather than judge our answers; simply be aware of what thoughts and feelings arise when we consider some tough questions.) For example: What are the deeper reasons, the messy stuff of vulnerability and broken promises, for wanting to lose weight or create wealth? Are your reasons based on fears of poor past performance or the confidence in seeing a larger vision of yourself come to life? And, an even better question: Will you accept the new you, be it slimmer of body or bulkier of wallet, despite any new challenges to this emerging chrysalis? Will you surrender your past stories of inadequacy to allow newer, perhaps shadowy, stories to emerge, to gain traction? This place, this spacious awareness within – part dream, part nightmare – is currently unknown but most certainly knowable. It is the passion of what's most essential to you cracking through the egg where it has been incubating. It is the light of your life's purpose seeping through the cracks of your socialization. So claim this deeper truth which is full of energy, full of meaning. Getting excited at the possibilities that await? Good. However, this great opportunity, tailor made just for you, doesn't come without a price.

Recognizing Our Outer Wholeness to Learning

The most obvious cost of change is the disruption of your stability. It can be uncomfortable or scary or perhaps even dangerous to leave the comforts and security of your semi-functioning (or dysfunctional) worldview. Of course we want to make our dreams come true. But wanting it is not enough to realize your goal. Neither is relying on someone else's plan, conveniently offered by a book or video or conference. Again these prompts are necessary but not sufficient. They are only the first steps in the change process. Let's use a baseball analogy. Identifying your needs and clarifying your promise may get you to first base. But will inspiring self-talk get you to home plate? The authors of this book are uneasy with the shallow approach taken by most "change plans" in the self-improvement industry. Their prolific products and services do heighten awareness and offer an intervention unique to their program. However, can they reliably and consistently bring the baserunner home to score a run? For the short term, maybe. For the long haul, probably not. Why? In our estimation that they don't adequately address the unasked question after everyone leaves the exciting seminar, "What do I do on Monday when I get back to my everyday life?" We take a different approach by creating a toolbox to practice the first footsteps of your purpose and passion given your limited time and resources. The tools from that toolbox come from many disciplines. They provide an instruction manual entitled

"Reflection" to increase your learning capacity. Then students can trust their instincts and take risks to follow their own hunches. Our approach is about the "process" of learning. We offer an education model to capture the momentum that gets you to first base with recontextualizations that advance you along to second and third base and eventually home to score a run.

Most of the self-help practitioners come from the fields of psychology, theology or business leadership. Their expertise is grounded in the long tradition of empirical science, religious scholarship or marketplace success. Compelling stuff, for sure. What could we educators add that's new or helpful? It is fair to ask us about the source of our authority to contribute to positive change in a meaningful way. Here's our bottom line: we believe that an education model deepens personal and interpersonal relationships. It expands the notion of your individual potential and – at the same time – deepens the connection to your primary community. We can offer time-tested "best-practice" applications that provide a better buoy in the choppy waters of the change process. From our wide background in K-12 classrooms, higher education in both undergraduate and graduate programs (face-to-face and online and hybrid/blended), partner and family counseling and mediation, plus lots and lots of trial and error, we've learned what it takes to help folks succeed. For us, too much of the self-help movement feels like drive-by transformation. In our experience, a one-shot intervention (via books, media, workshops, etc.) is simply not enough to change perceptions and long-ingrained habits. So, what can our approach do? We want to add several educational applications: 1) understanding the context of the proposed change, 2) developing a practice schedule to increasingly fine tune the adaptation of new behaviors, and 3) incorporating tools that use whole learning strategies which can provide effective knowledge and skills when first efforts don't succeed. Our approach is grounded in Albert Bandura's social learning theory which asserts that learning is more than behavioral responses governed solely by reinforcement. Our assumption is that learning is a *cognitive* process which takes place in a social setting. Learning becomes mindful in two specific ways: by observing a (hopefully positive) behavior to mimic and by observing the consequences of that particular behavior. In other words, learning happens through observation or direct instruction *and* through the observation of incentives and disincentives on what is being learned. This type of learning considers the internal processes (such as attention and motivation) affecting the learner. In this model the learner is not a passive recipient of information; he or she is an active agent in the construction of new beliefs and habits. We recognize that sustainable change is a complex and untidy affair. We are used to the messy cycle of hope, disappointment and eventual success inherent in the educational model. It's the stuff of miracle testimonials from our students. It's what keeps us in the game. So how do we "do" the cognitive process of social learning? We offer two responses: the first covers *curriculum* development and the second is about a model of *instructional* design.

Curriculum development

Curriculum development is the "what" of learning. Various approaches have been used to develop curricula, however, most incorporate these four features: *analysis* (What's the need or task?), *design* (What are the objectives?), *intervention* (What are the methods to teach the new learning?) and *evaluation* (How will progress be measured?). We've reduced this process to the ABCs of learning. Embedded in each modality is a specific application we have labeled the "Key 3:" Empathy, Grit and Growth Mindset. The descriptions below offer the yin and yang of how to unpack new knowledge and skill and attitude.

1. **A**FFECTIVE – <u>Heart:</u> *our emotions, feelings, intuitions, perceptions or moods*

   - <u>Empathy</u> connects us to our heart. If we can get past the "monkey mind" in our head and be curious to how others are responding to a situation, we are practicing empathy by demonstrating an understanding and sensitivity of another's mental state. It involves two components: a cognitive understanding of why someone is feeling a particular way and an emotional component of reacting to another person's emotional response. When we turn empathy inward we practice a self-compassion which can reduce emotional barriers to new and unfamiliar change and allow the transformative process to unfold.

2. BEHAVIORAL – Body/*Performance:* *observable activity; a pattern of action*

- Grit connects us to our body and movement. If we can believe, really believe, in a new image of our self, we are practicing grit. Creating a vision of new attitudes and behaviors toward an old nemesis allows us to stay in the present. By simply acknowledging but not identifying with my demons (ex: negative body image, feelings of financial insecurity, a sense of personal inadequacy in romantic or professional relationship, etc.) sidesteps harsh judgment. Grit focuses on perseverance and passion for long-term goals. Our behavioral homework is to increase stamina and to maintain effort despite potential setbacks. Grit turned inward is the practice of continual vigor toward a goal and knowing how to get up (after a setback) when you want to give up.

3. COGNITIVE – *Mind: perception, memory, judgment, and reasoning; knowing*

- Growth Mindset connects us to our mind. It is a bottom-line understanding that intelligence can be developed. Those with a "fixed mindset" believe that abilities are mostly innate and interpret failure as the lack of necessary basic aptitude. Those with a "growth mindset" believe that they can acquire any given ability provided they invest effort or study. While elements of our personality, such as sensitivity to mistakes and setbacks, can make us predisposed towards holding a certain mindset, we are able to reshape our mindset through our interactions. Growth mindset turned inward reframes a daunting task into an interesting game of how work and effort eventually leads to proficiency.

The ABCs of the Key 3 are necessary but hardly sufficient. They are merely props on an empty stage. The real electricity happens when the stage comes alive with actors and lighting and sound and the palpable energy of audience engagement. Likewise, growth to the more vibrant "you" occurs when all the moving parts are in sync. Just as the members of the audience momentarily suspend belief to allow the reality on stage to capture their imagination, the authors of this book ask you to suspend self-judgment of your deficits or limitations and imagine a different set of beliefs, grounded in a sense of abundant wonder. But that's only the first step, just getting on base. To get to home plate we need to be attentive in doing the work of transformation. It takes at least 45 days of conscious attention to change a belief (and longer depending upon our age and at when the limiting belief got instilled). This is the coaching phase of our program. In your daily practice you must consistently challenge the old belief and repeat the new one and monitor evidence pointing to the new belief and how it drives new behavior. The Key three – Empathy, Grit and Growth Mindset – are your vehicle to round the bases. New habits of mind can instill new behaviors by creating fresh options and having an attitude of play (remember, the fans and the sportscaster comment on an exciting "play" going down).

The ABCs represents a holistic way to address our basic needs through our heart, hand and head. People process information in countless different ways. If you are a global thinker, wanting to see the big picture before committing to a course of action, then you can focus on one specific element of the ABCs to solve your problem of change. Perhaps you are a thinker (Cognitive) and need to conceptualize a plan and a positive attitude (Growth Mindset) to achieve your change goal. Perhaps you are a feeling person (Affective) who can deeply empathize with the personal struggle of someone who has reached a formerly impossible dream. Perhaps you are an action person (Behavioral) who has keen powers of concentration (or stubbornness) to continue, one foot after another, to a new projected goal. It's important to remember that there is no best component of the ABCs. Think of how you overcame obstacles to meet a past challenge, whether it was learning how to drive a car or learning how to be a responsive parent. It's probably safe to assume that sometimes you found success by using your head and other times by leading with your heart. Who knows, you might have mixed and matched and used two modalities of the ABCs to get to the Promised Land. The key to practicing the ABCs of learning is doing what works for you at a given moment of time.

Instructional design

Instructional design is the "how" of learning. What instructional experiences can make learning new knowledge or skills more effective and appealing? The process is informed by pedagogy (theories of teaching) and andragogy (theories of adult learning) through various modes: student-only, teacher-led or community-based settings. There are many instructional design models but many are based on the ADDIE model with five phases: analysis, design, development, implementation, and evaluation. We have reduced this process to a three-step series:

1. WHAT? This phase identifies the *awareness* of what is to be learned: What's the problem? What was done in the past that worked? What was done in the past that didn't work? What new commitments can be made?

2. SO WHAT? This phase identifies the *intervention* of what is to be learned: What's your personal learning style? How do you process new information (Hearing, Seeing or Doing)? How do you learn best in a social context (in isolation *or* with another person *or* in a small group setting *or* in large groups *or* by using technology)? Additionally, how many repetitions of new information or skill is necessary to make it routine?

3. NOW WHAT? This phase identifies the *assessment* of what is to be learned: What is useful? What defines accountability, i.e. assessing emotional and social progress as well as cognitive change? What means are used to evaluate outcomes (tests, essays, presentations, performances, etc.)? What's in the gray area that can't be evaluated, i.e. what are leading trends or patterns of new behavior?

Listening to Our Inner Quiet

Traditional education is designed to train the mind. A more progressive education involving whole learning can effectively do two things: transfer knowledge and develop skills. However, these twins on the learning continuum are not enough to get the job done for sustainable change. Despite the mind's ability to recall, comprehend, analyze, synthesize, evaluate and create, it still can be trapped in a conceptual prison. Our thoughts -how we interpret our life or someone else's life or judge a situation –are no more than one viewpoint in the unified whole of reality. While the thinking mind can be a useful tool, it can also be very limiting when it gets too bossy. Have you ever had a moment when you realized that your mind's insistence on the familiar and past formulas for success were actually getting in the way for the new change to occur? It can be daunting and humbling to realize that the mind is only a part of the consciousness you are. For example, what is wisdom? Is it a high-end kind of thought? Not really. Wisdom becomes truly apparent from a shift in consciousness. It goes beyond thought; it arises when we give someone our full attention in a heightened field of awareness. What does this have to do with following dreams or changing habits? Why is it important to go beyond the thinking mind? Einstein had the perfect answer: "We cannot solve our problems with the same thinking we used when we created them." So how do we think anew about thinking? Another vital tool in your toolbox for sustainable change is paying attention to the lens of how we process information, of how we shift our consciousness.

As theologians and poets and singers attest, we have a better chance to shift our consciousness when we replace active mind with quiet mind. To further our previous example: wisdom bubbles up when we are still, simply looking and listening without a predetermined agenda. We access our wisdom when we allow ourselves to be deeply quiet, silent and still. The theologian Paul Tillich once observed that our world and ourselves would be changed for the better if we would seek "more rest for the soul." If we are really serious about making real changes in our life (and in our world) we have to quiet the inner noise, the "monkey mind," of our thinking. Regular periods of silence in our daily routine allow us to take that scary step toward personal responsibility for our actions by activating the intuition and imagination of our subconscious mind. Getting in touch with our inner quiet awakens new possibilities of responding to seemingly intractable challenges. Stillness is where creativity and solutions to problems are found. From this vast reservoir a new consciousness is born, weaving fragments of old ways of being with a newly emerging sense of self. This new consciousness represents a shift from "either/or" thinking to "both/and" thinking. When we move our attention to the wholeness right in front of us (fear *and* love, resistance *and* nonresistance, resentment *and* forgiveness, etc.) we can expand the options of outcomes available to us and fine tune the mindset with which we interpret our reality.

Focusing on the touchstone of our quiet nature is a key to tapping the abundant potential within us and with our world. It is the keyhole to sustainable change, paradoxically, it's invisible in plain sight. But here's the tricky part. What do we focus on to tap that inner wellspring? Ironically, that focus came when we embraced our perceived limitations. As we exchanged our back stories while writing this book, the authors recognized a truly perverse truth: when we acknowledge our vulnerability, honestly and without judgment, we found our deeper strength in an inner wholeness. So many times one of us would stare at the other in disbelief and say, "Really . . . I thought I was the only person in the world to have such feelings." These revelations are important way stations on our journey to transformation. We want to share our mistakes and triumphs as we've come to terms with the necessary potholes on the road to change. In the last section of each chapter the author's will share their own "vulnerability" stories as we struggled to resolve personal conflicts in our life. This process of removing the self-imposed boulders in our way is hard work. There's no playbook. And we're all in this together. It would be incredibly shortsighted and inauthentic to suggest changes toward sustainability without sharing our own "muddling through" process. We hope to stimulate a virtual dialogue by passing tidbits of our "aha" moments as we discovered the seeds of what's most alive in our lives.

The Last Word

We've come full circle. How do we take the leap to the new life we want? By showing up and learning how to build personal capacity. By embracing an educational model of outer wholeness and inner quiet. By holding sacred our hidden vitality. The mythologist Joseph Campbell nailed this truth: "I don't believe people are looking for the meaning of life as much as they are looking for the experience of being alive." We hope to offer this fulsome experience of being alive through overlapping strands: cross-disciplinary knowledge and the ABCs of expanding your personal toolbox and best practice applications of the Key 3 (empathy, grit and growth mindset) in a community learning environment . . . and, of course, quieting our ever-active mind. This is how we can get unstuck and reclaim our Light. This is the "juice" of our calling.

A final caveat. In our collective experience – 60 years of teaching between us – we've had remarkable success at helping students increase their confidence. They truly believe they can make sustainable change. Are the results guaranteed? No. Would another recipe for intervention work just as well? Perhaps. So, why invest in this approach? If you look at the table of contents you'll see that we there is no content to ensure a particular outcome. There is no specific information on how to lose weight or how to make money or how to raise children. Rather we are advocating "process" skills to help you construct a new paradigm or worldview that will increase the likelihood of personal change (or systems change, for that matter). Think of this process knowledge as a toolkit to increase your confidence in taking on long-avoided challenges. This is hardly a popular remedy because it demands a leap of faith and a willingness to make lots of mistakes until you find the right combination of the Key 3 that makes sense to you. And, making matters even scarier, we suggest that you share your journey of discovery with others, in community, especially during the messy moments. This approach works, but only if you work it. Fear not what lies ahead. We will companion with you. We have taken our own medicine and will share some of our own stories of how we worked with the Key 3 to turn the gristle of our barriers into the greatness of our bounty. It's time for the reenergized you to show up. If you are ready, let's get to it!

Chapter 2

Home Plate – Identifying Our Needs

"You can't always get what you want, but sometimes you might find, you get what you need." Mick Jagger

One of my [WB] first jobs was as a counselor for a national weight loss franchise. I would hold half-hour weekly sessions on healthy eating habits, positive self-image and proactive behavioral tactics to prepare my charges for when the evil binge gnome made an appearance (usually during festive times like going out to eat or holiday celebrations). Yet, in my opinion, we started the weight-loss process on the wrong foot; we focused on their wants more than their needs. Before I met them our sales team already asked them how many pounds they *wanted* to lose and why they *wanted* to lose the weight. A great majority of these weight loss customers were women and they nearly always had a quick response, a desired end result: to fit into a lower-size wedding dress, to be able to wear a bikini for a summer vacation, to look fabulous for a family reunion. However, they had more difficulty when I asked them nearly the same question, a *process* question, in the counseling room: why did they *need* to lose the weight? Better put, what *needs* were not being met at their current weight? A lot of awkward silence and squirming generally followed my questions. It was incredibly painful for them to identify the real needs that motivated them to spend time and money to lose weight. A surprising number admitted that no one from their immediate circle had asked them that question before. Initially, I was startled. Why? What might happen if you opened up and revealed what you really needed? However, after hearing the same story told again and again, with a different cast of characters or in a different setting, I began to see a pattern: "loving women," that is, women who care for others more than themselves, have no needs. (The analog for men was: "standup men," that is, guys who didn't want to appear weak, had no needs.) What is this craziness, I thought, which prevented someone from sharing a genuine human need? They all had the same answer. They were afraid that they would be judged harshly if they were open and honest. They were scared that a significant other in their life would reject them, tell them what's wrong with them, that they were too sensitive or needy or demanding or _____ (fill in the blank). The message was plain. It's better to be oblivious to our needs than have to deal with the pain behind it. Silent suffering seemed preferable than having to deal with a negative opinion from family or friends who disapprove of such aberrant behavior. Given these challenges, how can authentic needs be verbalized without prompting a reactive "like/dislike" response?

ABCs of Noting Needs: Affective

From Hard-Hearted to Soft-Hearted Awareness

If deep change is really going to take hold we need to die to our past understanding of success and enter a new world of being. This new world of well-being starts when we soften our heart and cultivate prosperity thinking. This means being ruthless but not harsh in examining deeper beliefs about ourselves and our world. A hard-hearted awareness focuses on deficit thinking; the voices in our head are what we heard from significant others *from our past*: "you are too fat, "you are too skinny," "you are too bookish," you are too dumb," "you are too controlling," "you are too lazy," etc. The childhood adage "sticks and stones can break my bones but words can never hurt me" is just plain wrong. Words from someone we trust can pierce through a well-armored heart. In the face of certain condemnation it takes loads of courage to take a risk to open one's heart and be vulnerable.

On the other hand, a soft-hearted awareness focuses on abundance thinking; the voices in our head are from our own awakening *in this present moment*. Perhaps they are the faint whispers from our childhood yearnings, perhaps they emerge from the wellspring of our imagination: "you are strong and sturdy," "you are slender and flexible," "you are a good problem-solver," "you are thoughtful and intuitive," "you are a person of action," "you are observant and reflective," etc. It's all perception, right?

Given entrenched beliefs and habits, how can we move from "either/or" thinking to "both/and" thinking? The trick, of course, is accepting both versions of the heart simultaneously, even if it's only for a moment. How can this be possible?

Guided Imagery

The pathway between these two worlds has been known for ages. We practice it whenever we take a long deep breath to calm ourselves. This elixir is something we've known about it, in concept at least, all our lives. It is the practice of meditation. Meditation is what we do to dial down our mind, away from outer concerns towards an inner condition of spacious awareness. It's one of the best tools we have to balance our emotions, soothe our physical discomfort and become attentive to the peace of the present moment. Meditation trains the mind to acknowledge its content without becoming identified with that content. But it's often too challenging to meditate without a formal practice or teacher. One useful alternative is to do guided imagery. This involves listening to a practitioner (or from a prerecorded meditation on audio or video tape) who sets a tone that allows you to imagine an alternative perspective. Meditation allows for that cooped-up sigh to be released. In that moment of expanded awareness you can mentally let go of unproductive thoughts and behaviors and rehearse strategies to increase your coping skills. Skillful meditators on an audio meditation literally walk you through a process which results in a calm and peaceful state. In this relaxed place your mind is more open to accepting new mental imagery.

We can recommend two excellent online audio sources for guided meditation. The first comes from Chopra Center for Wellbeing (http://www.chopra.com/ccl/guided-meditations). Through a variety of offerings the listener can shift to a place of "balance, healing, transformation, and the expansion of awareness." Another excellent series of guided meditations comes from Tara Brach (https://www.tarabrach.com/guided-meditations/), who blends Western psychology with Eastern spiritual practices. Her meditations balance a mindful attention to our inner life and a compassionate engagement with our world. Hint: guided meditations offer an array of gateways. Pick a topic that resonates with your most immediate need (ex: healing, dreaming, gratitude, letting go of control, awaking abundance, etc.) and do it often enough to get the desired result. These audio versions generally last about ten minutes. Many people begin and end their day listening to a guided meditation. Either solo meditation or guided meditation can help us feel the contours of our needs without becoming enslaved to them. A little goes a long way! Caveat emptor: the realization of benefits can be subtle and invigorating!

ABCs of Noting Needs: **B**ehavioral

Okay, let's take stock. Assuming that you feel empowered enough to open your heart a crack and entertain the possibility of softening some core beliefs around your affective nature, what temporary scaffolding can be erected to accommodate the changes? Think of this structure as an electronic game, invisible to others, that allows you to make plans to fill the gap between your present state (what is) and your desired state (what can be). The name of this game is PNA or personal needs assessment. The first step in making an attitude adjustment is to dream about new realities. The second step is to scheme for those realities. A personal needs assessment puts those fragmentary dreams into a concrete organizer that focuses on decisions about specific outcomes.

Here's the plan to make more informed decisions:

1. define, specifically, your need;
2. gather and analyze relevant data to create new routines;
3. set priorities and determine criteria to evaluate success;
4. establish a schedule of sub deadlines and incentives.

So let's take this model for a spin around the block. One popular needs assessment is the SWOT analysis which is often used as a planning or review process in education, business or governmental settings. SWOT stands for Strengths, Weaknesses, Opportunities, and Threats. The basic process involves gathering information about an organization's activities and outcomes within a set time period. A simplified version of the SWOT process might involve these steps:

1. Members representing different interests of an organization share celebrations and concerns for several meetings, each lasting a minimum of 90 minutes;

2. A list of successes and failures of the organization over the past year is generated. Limited discussion follows, focusing on understanding what's really going on but not dwelling too long on any one feature;

3. Based on the understanding of the organization's strengths and weaknesses, members develop a list of external environment's opportunities and threats;

4. Members brainstorm ideas for maximizing strengths and minimizing weaknesses by taking advantage of opportunities and neutralizing threats.

A needs assessment can also be used as a planning process for individual outcomes as well as assessing organizational needs. For example, imagine using the SWOT approach to weight loss: identify a specific goal (lose 25 – 30 pounds), gather information from a variety of sources (from MDs, nutritionists, exercise coaches as well those who know your weight yo-yo history), identify strengths and weaknesses (what worked and didn't work in the past), determine criteria for success (what new opportunities you will now embrace and what you intend to do when an obstacle or threat occurs), and finally, making a decision of what an acceptable outcome looks like, without dwelling on whether or not you achieved everything from your original goal. And, of course, celebrate any new attitudes or behaviors that now become a routine part of your life!

ABCs of Noting Needs: Cognitive

A final stock-taking. If you are willing to allow yourself a "both/and" perspective of conflicting feelings toward change and you have a sound plan to reach your goals for hard-to-change needs, then that's that, right? Why would you need anything more? And you would be right . . . for the short term at least. What happens, however, when (and it's "when," not "if") you relapse. What will you do when an unforeseen obstacle becomes bigger than your imagined strategy to overcome it? To prepare for these nasty little surprises, it's time to introduce you to your very own superhero, ingeniously disguised as an unwelcomed curse. It's none other than – tah dah – Question Man! Asking questions about foreboding challenges is your flashlight in the darkness. The process of questioning is one of the most basic and profound learning tools at your disposal. Asking a focused question is one of the ways to bring enhanced awareness to those tattered moments of disappointment, when you've fallen off the wagon. Questioning exposes our basic curiosity, our innate desire to know how something works. It's that spirit of questioning that led to Maslow's hierarchy of needs.

In 1943, Abraham Maslow, a developmental psychologist, published a paper describing how human motivations move through a particular pattern. He identified a hierarchy of needs, represented as a pyramid with the more basic needs at the bottom and the highest needs of self-actualization at the top. (An aside: the hierarchy is generally represented as a pyramid; however, Maslow never used this graphic to represent the different levels.) The bottom four layers of the pyramid contain the most basic levels of human needs. These needs must be met before the individual will strongly desire the secondary or higher level needs. He labeled these fundamental needs of esteem, friendship and love, security, and physical needs, as "deficiency" needs; if these needs are not met the individual will feel anxious and tense. Yet Maslow also recognized the human need to go past self-interest. He coined the term "metamotivation" to describe the motivation of people who go beyond the scope of the basic needs and strive for constant betterment. In his later years, Maslow explored a further dimension of needs with **self-transcendence at the top.** At this level, the self only finds its actualization in giving itself to some higher goal outside oneself, in altruism and spirituality.

Maslow's hierarchy of needs

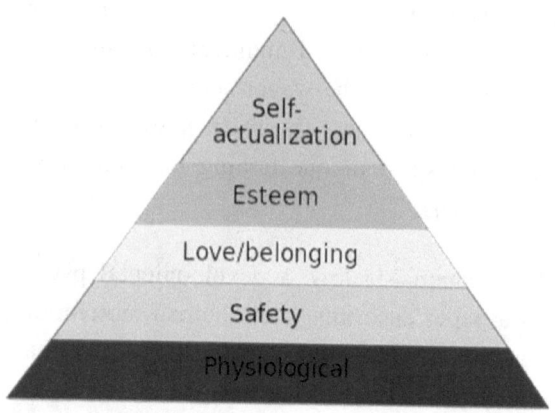

One: Physical/Survival Needs

Food, water, air, sex and sleep are primary needs. These needs must be met before any other needs are met. When our physical/survival needs are not met it creates extreme and *rational* fear. Our most primitive or basic fear is dying.

Level Two: Safety/Security Needs

Protection from physical elements (cold, heat, wind, rain) and freedom from fear of harm to our bodies, minds and emotions are safety/security needs. Humans have a need for structure, order and personal boundaries. Routines and rituals keep us feeling safe and secure.

Level Three: Love/Social Needs

The need for love is both a psychological and physical. A need for affection is also a need to belong. When we identify with a group, the group helps define who we are. An example would be the origin of our family name or our political affiliation.

Level Four: Appreciation/Self-Esteem Needs

The need to achieve, to be productive, to master skills all lead to a healthy sense of competence. Recognition from others for achievements lead to feelings of self-worth, self-love and self-confidence.

Level Five: Self-Actualization Needs

The need to recognize self-worth, potential and the value each person brings to a greater global community is self-actualization. When one takes full accountability or the needs, thoughts and feelings of themselves and others, they become centered, balanced, and able to show the highest form of intellect; empathy.

The human brain is complex. Many different motivations from various levels of Maslow's hierarchy can occur at the same time. Maslow spoke clearly about these levels and their satisfaction in terms such as "relative," "general," and "primary." Instead of stating that the individual focuses on a certain need at any given time, Maslow stated that a certain need "dominates" the human organism at a particular moment. Thus Maslow acknowledged the likelihood that the different levels of motivation could occur at any time in the human mind, but the hierarchy focuses on identifying the basic types of motivation and the order in which they should be met.

That said, we advocate using questioning to target a particular need by bringing conscious awareness to the perceived deficiency. For instance, if a reorganization at work causes a demotion and reduces monthly income for the primary provider, it would affect each member of the family differently. The chief breadwinner might feel challenged at level 4 and ask "How can I be more productive to feel a healthy sense of competence?" The chief caretaker might feel challenged at level 2 or 3, wondering, "How can I protect my family from potential physical and psychological shortages?" The change in family dynamics might also affect the children adversely. If routines change abruptly, they may become anxious or have irrational fears characteristic of Level 1:"How come Daddy (or Mommy) isn't home at night like (s)he used to be? Does that mean (s)he doesn't love me anymore?"

Needs come from a more shadowy place than wants. I [WB] conducted an interesting lesson on wants and needs with my college students who were preparing to become elementary school teachers. I put them in groups of four at six separate tables. An envelope was on each table with slips of paper inside describing a particular item or activity (ex: milk, chocolate milk, pencil, computer, going to elementary school, going to college, etc.). They had to create a T Chart with Wants as one heading and Needs as the other heading. Their job was to discuss and then place each slip of paper under one of the two headings. However, they had to reach group consensus before they made their selection. At the end of this task they had to draft a definition of wants and needs to which they all could agree. As you might have guessed, the activity produced a loud and raucous exchange. The lesson ended with a class discussion on the criteria for perceiving a want or a need. My personal favorite: "a need is something you gotta have, no questions asked."

A final point, or, at least a fine point – on the line between wants and needs. Heaped on top of our need to survive are hundreds of wants masquerading as needs in our mind. Robin Wall Kimmerer, a Native American member of the Citizen Potawatomi Nation and a Distinguished Professor of Botany at New York's SUNY College of Environmental Science and Forestry introduces the teaching of Honorable Harvest with her students to identify needs and how to separate them from wants. She offers a non-exploitative way to maintain vitality in our natural and built worlds: "The Honorable Harvest tells us to take only what we need and never more than half of what's available, to use everything that we take, to minimize the harm that is done, to share what we've taken, and to be grateful, always giving something back in return." This traditional wisdom reinforces the concept of what is mutually beneficial. This prescription for sustainability is also an appropriate model to explain how we expand our awareness of a basic need by quieting the mind.

Listening to Our Inner Quiet

How can we quiet our mind to discern the magnetic pull of wants and needs? The first step is to pay attention to how thoughts arise. The mind can play tricks on us because it is constantly hungry for food. It is not only insatiably on the hunt for food for thought but also food for identity. The mind's appetite is voracious; it feeds on the food of our ego. Every time you say "I" or "me," you are referring to the ongoing story of your life, your likes and dislikes, your fears and desires. This sense of who we are is conditioned by the past deeds and future hopes. Since it is not anchored in the present it is rarely satisfied for very long. When the thoughts in your head command your undivided attention it really means you are becoming invested in a house of cards of your own making. That voice in your head never stops speaking. The constant parade of thoughts is the ego speaking, a mind-made construction of "me," protected by your unconscious sense of self. When you notice that voice and respond to the cascading thoughts *nonjudgmentally* it's easier to pay attention to the energy around the thoughts. For example, "I am so frustrated by my boss when . . ." can become "frustrating thought arising, stage left. Take a deep breath or two and let it go." When I give my full attention to this moment (and not digress to an obsessive retelling of past grievances or fantasize about future relief from a suffering) I can break out of my self-constructed ego jail. Intentionally focusing on my inner quiet – taking a walk, doing tai chi or yoga, practicing conscious breathing – puts me smack dab in the present moment. In the midst of a deepening stillness, my mindset shifts. I can consciously choose how to respond to those persnickety wants bubbling up. Being aware of right now, this very minute, can free me up to more fully address my condition – what I really need – without a whole lot of emotional baggage. Whew! What a relief.

Wayne's story

I'm a foodie, a card carrying member of an informal but universal club of narcissists. I came by my affliction honestly. My mother, born and bred during the Great

Depression, felt compelled to make sure her children had enough to eat . . . even if they weren't hungry. Her unrelenting focus on food security reached legendary status in my family. She perfected what she called the "dart technique." Whenever an unsuspecting victim had his or her mouth open (my sibs and I were a talkative lot so that was often) she deftly applied a blitzkrieg maneuver and stuffed our gullet with half-inch squares of bologna. To this day I hate bologna! Unfortunately, a habit of a want-disguised-as-a-need took hold. Food is both my sustenance and addiction. Whenever I feel blue there will ALWAYS be something from the pantry or fridge to sooth my tattered nerves. Properly speaking, my problem is not with food itself but with mindless bingeing of food. The process is invariable: Something upsets me and – Bam! – the switch to my volition suddenly shuts down. My mind just clicks off and I totally absolve myself of any responsibility of what my body does next. So, of course, overeating became the norm. I've struggled with my weight and body-image nearly all my adult life. Regretfully, I've passed on these impulsive habits to my children. Even after several abdominal surgeries, it's still an effort to limit the portion size of my favorite foods. So what's my Rx? I don't know, it's still a work in progress. Here's my latest needs assessment to limit portion size. I call it the 20/20 plan. Twenty minutes into a meal, I stop eating, and ask out loud if my hunger has been satisfied. Then I wait for 20 minutes (drinking water allowed) before I answer the question. If I am still physically hungry I can eat, albeit slowly. If I am psychologically hungry, I wait another 20 minutes (drinking water expected) before answering another set of questions: "Where am I on the Maslow's Hierarchy?" and "What non-food remedy would plug the need?" Does my plan work? Honest answer: good days and bad days. What encourages me, however, is that I am becoming more conscious of my behavior and I shut down less often than before. Truth be told, I am both glad and sad at my progress, glad that I am gaining control of my life and sad that it has taken me this long to put the brakes on. Sigh.

<u>Barb's story</u>

I have been obsessed with my physical appearance my entire life. Being a dancer for over two decades meant a fine tuning of what a dancer's body should look and feel like. One extra ounce on my frame and I could not get my leg as high in ballet class or be centered for that triple turn. It was palpable. The good thing is that I never turned to eating disorders or use of diet pills. I did not always eat what was best or enough to really sustain my dancing body as a healthy machine. We live in such an appearance-obsessed world. Stand in line at any grocery store checkout and you'll see magazines graced with the latest Hollywood stars or famous people who all look fabulous and un-aged. This is not reality. Photoshop is an amazing tool but one that threatens our perception of real life, real issues, and yes, real bodies and faces. We are a quick fix society and want the youthful look now and forever. Healthy eating tips are standard fare during cooking demonstrations on television talk shows. Exercise classes abound. The plastic surgery industry has taken on a life of its own. My cognitive, rational brain knows this well. However, my heart and emotional brain lean too far in the opposite direction way too often. Do I eat like a bird on many days? Absolutely. Do I obsess over one more walk in the day just to take off more fat cells? You bet. In thinking about wants and needs it is important to ask the big and unnerving question, Can I be healthy, and happy? It took a tragedy for me to see how much I take good health for granted. When a dear friend was paralyzed in a biking accident a few years ago, it shattered my world. A once vibrant friend lost his ability to do simple tasks. Being obsessed with my looks seemed so trivial in the face of his life-changing accident. My superficial wants turned into deeply felt needs. I kicked body obsession out of my life. I developed more gratitude for what I have and can do with my current body. Do I still struggle with the 'look?' Yes, I probably always will. However, now when I look at Maslow's Hierarchy I am drawn toward the need of love for others and an appreciation for a strong self-esteem. Healthy living comes from making good decisions, especially around the value of a healthy and strong body, not one that must 'look' good.

Chapter 3

First Base – Empathy:

Caring About Others To Promote Self-Care

"You never really understand another person until you consider things from his point of view – until you climb inside of his skin and walk around in it."   Harper Lee,
To Kill A Mockingbird

"I am he, as you are he, as you are me, and we are all together."   Beatles, I Am A Walrus

"Me. We."   A poem by Muhammad Ali

For over 11 years I [BH] have been a mediator in a court-referred family dispute center. Happily, the courts have recognized that issues of child custody are better resolved by parents than by judges or juries. Unfortunately, the prevailing "win/lose" mindset of the judicial system too often results in settlements rather than durable agreements. Regrettably, a large percentage of these settlements eventually fall apart. What's the difference between the two? A settlement represents a "power-over" outcome, accept my last offer or else. A durable agreement represents a "power-with" commitment to a win/win solution. The foundation of a durable agreement is mutuality in a relationship, for example, how can parents attend to the welfare of their child(ren) despite the bruised feelings between spouses? The trick of a seasoned mediator is to move the frame of reference of those in conflict from me to we. By listening fully for that mutual emotional space in each party, their nonverbal presence as well as their verbal exchange, a skillful mediator can shift a defensive monologue to a more productive dialogue. A vital key in mediation is to empower the disputants to recognize win/win possibilities even during a tense negotiation. How? By filling the empathy gap. Empathy involves under-standing and responding to the emotional states of other people. In a mediation there are so many ways to telegraph empathy, both verbally ("It's OK to feel this way.") and nonverbally (maintaining nonthreatening eye contact, physically leaning in, offering affirming gestures, etc.). There is a magic moment in mediation, called "getting to yes," when hard walls become tenuous bridges. It often occurs when I put my guard down long enough to allow the disputants to put their guard down too. In this place an awkward silence can dissolve into healing tears; name-calling can morph into sharing what's truly important. In that moment the disputants change the nature of their relationship from adversarial to non-adversarial, from non-supportive to empathetic. The tension in the room softens. For a brief moment they are able to put themselves in another's shoes and experience the events and emotions of the other person the way that person experienced them. They are exhibiting empathy.

Despite recent advances from neurological scientists and mindfulness studies from research psychologists, empathy can be easily misunderstood. Why? One possible culprit is our unconscious embrace of two divergent world views. From one lens the world is seen as a very scary place, full of lurking dangers: it's a dog-eat dog world so get yours before someone else does. From this perspective, self-interest is the common-sense bottom line. Think about how you respond to the hectic demands of your workplace in our competitive and deadline-driven post-industrial economy. Anger, alienation and anonymity fuel our attitude. However, another lens shows the world as a loving place, full of wonder and promise: do unto others as you want them to do unto you. . From this perspective, care for self and others is the bottom line. Think about a mother and father (and extended family and friends) with a new-born baby. History is strewn with examples of both perspectives. Examples of self-interest might include the 17th C English philosopher Thomas Hobbs ("life is nasty, brutish and short.") or the 19th C ideas of Charles Darwin's natural selection high-lighting innate human selfishness (although at the end of his life Darwin recognized and wrote about the benevolence of the human condition) to the mid-20th C novels of Ayn Rand emphasizing the primacy of individualism and isolation. These are instances of a Me-world with competition and aggression as the social norm. On the other hand, examples of altruism abound, whether it's a story of individual heroism or collective defiance of a people to unjust laws (from the 13th C uprising of British peasants which resulted in the Magna Carta to the 20th C nonviolent mass movements of Mahatma Gandhi and Martin Luther King which legalized civil rights for marginalized minorities). Here are instances of a We-world with cooperation and mutual reciprocity as the social norm.

Both conditions exist simultaneously within us as we vacillate between the competing priorities of attending to our own needs and being available to the needs of others. What are the risks and opportunities which influence each condition? It may be instructive to note that the lower four levels of Maslow's Hierarchy reflect a needs deficit; something is missing in an individual's life: clothing, shelter, safety, friendship, self-esteem, etc. However, at the highest level of Self-Actualization an individual focuses on assets more than deficits; one's highest needs are satisfied by relating meaningfully with others. When one takes full accountability of the needs, thoughts and feelings of themselves and others, they can balance their deficit and asset needs and demonstrate empathy. In fact, in his later years, Maslow identified "self-transcendence" as a more appropriate vision of the highest level of needs. The self only finds its actualization when it can give itself to some higher goal outside oneself, in altruism and spirituality. One of the ways we define our self is through the satisfying of our needs. How do we project our self onto others? How does the projected self of others become part of one's own self? How do experiences of both self and others play a role together? When is it more appropriate to use reason rather than emotion in dealing with a shaky engagement? Given this seesaw of responding to the needs of self and to the needs of others, how can empathy be appreciated without provoking a defensive or guilty reaction?

[Author's note: The Key 3 of Empathy, Grit and Growth Mindset are the foundation stones of our approach to shifting a stuck or fearful perception to a positive, pro-active outcomes. Therefore, given the application focus of Empathy, Grit and Growth Mindset we will use the instructional design template "What? So What? Now What?" in the next three chapters rather than the curriculum development template (ABCs of Affective, Behavioral and Cognitive). The rationale of each theme will be explored followed by a section on Inner Quiet and examples of how the authors are dealing with this character trait.]

The WHAT of Empathy

Empathy opens people up to unknown outcomes and a sense that goals and behaviors may change. To better understand the unpredictability of accepting different motivations (self vs. other) social scientists have settled on describing empathy from two perspectives: affective empathy or cognitive empathy. Affective empathy is the capacity to respond with appropriate feelings to the emotional state of another person. Sometimes called emotional contagion, affective empathy has a plus side and a minus side. Obviously there are benefits to both parties when someone shows care and compassion for another due to his or her suffering. However, without conscious awareness, affective empathy can be harmful to a sensitive soul who experiences personal discomfort and anxiety in response to another's suffering. Those individuals who are extremely empathic need to learn to manage their empathy through cognitive means in order to be clear and intentional about their gift (or curse).

Cognitive empathy is the largely conscious drive to accurately recognize and understand another's emotional state. Sometimes this kind of empathy is called perspective taking. When viewing a situation from another point of view a question is often asked: how is empathy different from sympathy or compassion? A sympathetic individual has feelings of care and understanding for someone in need but does not share his or her emotional state with the sufferer: "Oh, Dorothy's is hurting in a bad way. I feel so sorry for her predicament." A compassionate individual has feelings of care and understanding for someone in need and can share in their emotional state: "Oh Dorothy, I hear such pain in your voice." An empathetic individual is slightly different from a compassionate individual (although the jury is still out on this point) by being able to share and mirror another's emotions in both suffering and non-suffering moments: "Dorothy, I sense your pain. How unsettling. Just remember, I've got your back regardless . . . during the good, the bad and the ugly times."

Some of this empathic connection is physiological. In the last two decades neurological research has revealed mirror neurons, specific places in the brain that produce empathic responses. When we experience pain certain areas of the brain fire up. The same area of the brain also lights up when we see someone else going through the same experience. For instance, if we've seen someone stub their toe or fall off a bike we might wince because we could sense that pain ourselves. That wincing – that unconscious reaction – is caused by **mirror neurons** firing in our brains. And these same neurons fire whether the action happens to us or to someone we're watching. The discovery of mirror neurons was a significant breakthrough because it revealed that our brains have evolved in a way that enables us to recognize and understand the emotions and intentions of others – not just by thinking but actually *feeling*.

Brain researcher Simon Baron-Cohen points to a physiological explanation of empathy. About 10 brain areas have been connected to the empathy response including the medial prefrontal cortex, the orbito-frontal cortex and the frontal operculum. As our understanding of the human brain gets more and more sophisticated, medical researchers been able to pinpoint particular chemicals that are linked to certain kinds of behavior. For example, the brain chemical oxytocin plays a central role in social behaviors like bonding and empathy. It's often referred to as "the love hormone" and has been linked to higher levels of generosity. Neuroscientist Vilayanur Ramachandran has argued that these neurons allow us to learn complex social behaviors and has called them "the basis of civilization."

However, there is a down side; too much empathy can be harmful. If someone has a brain impairment the emotional connection with another person can become severely strained. For example, narcissism is a defect of affective but not cognitive empathy. A bipolar condition is a deficit in cognitive but not affective empathy. Autism and schizophrenia are deficits in both cognitive and affective empathy. Psychologist have labeled the "empathy trap" as an extremely toxic behavior. It's a negative perfect storm in a relationship where someone with pronounced antisocial tendencies preys on an individual with high levels of empathy in order to get his or her own way. The result:

bullying behavior from the predator and emotional paralysis from the victim.

So the question arises, what's a safe way to get the most out of affective empathy? The link between our mirror neuron system and brain dysfunction is still tentative. While neurological scientists and social psychologists explore the biochemistry of empathy we can also raise our awareness of self-care strategies to decrease affective burnout. We can ask ourselves about environmental factors that can give us some control of our cognitive empathy responses. For example, how were we nurtured in our family, schools and community? Or, how can I be more intentional in choosing where and when to act empathetically? Mirror neurons provide a biological basis for social intelligence by enabling deep emotional connectedness, mimicry, and cooperation. Over time they have contributed to our sense of morality. Yet a mature expression of empathy requires a conducive environment in which to experiment with lots and lots of practice to allow empathetic responses to become second nature.

The SO WHAT of Empathy

How does the understanding of another person's feeling translate to actual behavior? More specifically, how can we measure and predict a range of behavioral perspectives when it comes to empathy? One way to get a handle on the physical perception of empathy is to pay attention to body reactions. This means learning to read the cues of another person's emotional and social intelligence in the form of nonverbal behavior or gestures indicating specific relational behavior.

Researchers measure the behavioral aspects of empathy in three ways:

1) by recording the presence or absence of verbal cues that prompt a felt empathy. An individual will reach out to help another through emotionally charged words; alternatively, a felt empathy may be shown by recording the presence or absence of nonverbal cues;

2) by recording body or somatic measurements of an empathic exchange. This might be demonstrated through voice expression, facial reactions or temper-ature changes on the skin; or

3) through self-reporting surveys which detail feelings of empathy with another.

Although measuring empathy has been achieved through various questionnaires (ex: the Hogan Empathy Scale, the Balanced Emotional Empathy Scale, the Interpersonal Reactivity Index, and the Empathy Quotient) it's tricky to get an accurate picture of the inner state of an empathizer. Instead, role-taking thinking is reported: "If I were him, I'd . . . ." Nevertheless, most SEL (Social Emotional Learning) researchers believe that empathy is learnable. In a 2014 study Caroline Tisot and Teresa Monforte looked at environmental factors that developed empathy in young children. One significant result showed paternal warmth and involvement as a positive predictor of empathy development, particularly for sons. (Interestingly, in the same study, maternal warmth and involvement was negatively related to empathy development in girls. This finding seems odd since many scientific studies found females to be more empathetic than males.)

The "So-What?" question asks, "can empathy be taught and learned? According to Edith Stein, a German phenomenologist, empathy can be facilitated, interrupted and blocked, but it cannot be forced to occur. What makes empathy unique is that it happens to us indirectly. When empathy occurs, we find ourselves experiencing it, rather than directly causing it to happen. That makes the act of empathy unteachable through traditional didactic lessons. Instead, promoting attitudes and behaviors such as self-awareness, nonjudgmental positive regard for others, good listening skills, and self-confidence are important steps in generating empathic awareness.

Such skill-building in in empathy is rapidly becoming part of the required curriculum for teacher training. Currently teacher training programs focus on teacher dispositions. However, a movement is afoot to emphasize the teacher-student relationship. A consortium of local politicians and educators and social service leaders in Seattle recently published The Road Map Project to develop "Strategies for Building Motivation, Engagement & 21st Century Skills" for young people (Youth Development Executives of King County, 2014). They recommend balancing relationship-skills and interpersonal development with academic skills. The movement to teach affective skills alongside cognitive lessons is also evident at the student level of schooling. The Ashoka network of Changemaker Schools (https://startempathy.org/changemaker-schools/) are "making the development of empathy a priority in their curricula, culture, and systems" to support "children as change makers – individuals with the skill set and connection to purpose that enable them to generate ideas and take initiative to effectively solve problems and drive positive change."

Indeed, the jury is out about is empathy can be learned. However, the deeper question is this: "Can we tap into our full empathic potential in everyday life?" To answer that we have to learn how to develop empathic skills. Empathy is about paying attention to another human being, giving them our focus and asking 'what are they feeling?', 'why are the feeling this way?' and making a commitment to understand what is happening in their world. The soft skills of empathy are relatively straightforward to sketch out but slippery to enact. Here's a short-list of what to look for:

1) Pay attention – we all share similar feelings. Can we witness a felling in another person, however challenging, with curiosity rather than judgment?

2) Validate that feeling without editorializing i.e. *"I can see you're really angry"* rather than *"There's no need to be that angry."*

3) Practice compassion, with others and with yourself.

According to the latest neuroscience research, 98% of people (the exceptions include those with psychopathic tendencies) have the ability to empathize wired into their brains – an in-built capacity for stepping into the shoes of others and understanding their feelings and perspectives. The "Now What?" section will explore how boost our empathy level.

The NOW WHAT of Empathy

Almost everyone can learn to be more empathic, just like we can learn to ride a bike or drive a car. Start with a warm-up exercise. Simon Baron-Cohen suggests paying close attention to "reading the mind in the eyes." Given someone's "look" what word or words would you choose that best describes what that person is feeling or thinking. Going a step further, there are three simple but powerful strategies for unleashing the empathic potential that is latent in our neural circuitry.

1) Make a habit of "radical listening"

Marshall Rosenberg, psychologist and founder of Non-Violent Communication emphasizes the importance of "our ability to be present to what's really going on within – to the unique feelings and needs a person is experiencing at that very moment." Listening carefully for people's feelings and needs – whether it is a friend who has just been diagnosed with breast cancer or a spouse who is upset at you for working late yet again – gives them a sense of being understood. Let people have their say, hold back from interrupting and even reflect back what they've told you so they knew you were really listening. There's a term for doing this – "radical listening". Radical listening can have an extraordinary impact on resolving conflict situations. Rosenberg points out that in employer-employee disputes, if both sides literally repeat what the other side just said before speaking themselves, conflict resolution is reached 50% faster.

2) Look for the human behind everything

A second step is to deepen empathic concern for others by developing an awareness of all those individuals hidden behind the surface of our daily lives, on whom we may depend in some way. A Buddhist-inspired approach to this is to spend a whole day becoming mindful of every person connected to your routine actions. So when you have your morning coffee, think about the people who picked the coffee beans. As you button your shirt, consider the labor behind the label by asking yourself: "Who sewed on these buttons? Where in the world are they? What are their lives like?" Then continue throughout the day, bringing this curiosity to who is driving the train, vacuuming the office floor or stacking the supermarket shelves. It is precisely such mindful awareness that can spark empathic action on the behalf of others, whether it's buying Fairtrade coffee or becoming friends with the office cleaner. It's about recovering the curiosity everyone had as children, but which society is so good at beating out of us. Get beyond superficial talk but beware of interrogating people. Respect the advice of oral historian Studs Terkel – who always spoke to people on the bus on his daily commute: "Don't be an examiner, be the interested inquirer."

3) Practice living in someone's shoes through perspective-taking or fantasy

Perspective-taking happens most directly when an individual consciously adopts the psychological perspective of another person. An example: When encountering his harried wife after work, an empathetic husband might say: "I can see how frazzled you are after doing too many errands with the kids today. Your face looks tense and your voice sounds sharp. I totally get it. I felt totally drained last Saturday when I took them with me to the hardware store and that was only a 45 minutes trip." Note the process. Instead of immediately arguing for his own needs (which makes sense since he is probably tired from his day at work and restrains an initial impulse to vent his own frustrations) he gives a both/and response. He makes an observation of the situation, shares a feeling in a nonjudgmental tone, and identifies with his wife's distress by echoing a similar perspective. This moment of empathic concern can immediately de-escalate combustible tensions ready to explode.

Another way to show perspective-taking can happen through a flight of fantasy. Think of a teenager who takes comfort in sci-fi movies or electronic games or in romantic fantasy novels to ward off perceived alienation and despair. By constructing an alternate reality they can indirectly identify with the plight of the protagonists (or antagonists). An imaginative empathy can manifest through an "if-then" impulse. The adolescent who feels besieged by demanding adults requiring homework to be completed or clothes to be put away can find satisfaction in the world of his or her mind: "Aaah, my light saber will protect me from these vile demons!" Studies have shown that perspective-taking ability tends to work better with adults and fantasy play works well with children. The key for both is to imagine themselves in another place or situation about how people are likely to act in a particular situation.

Empathy in Relationships: I and Thou

The consciousness necessary for empathy to be activated is very similar to the ideas of the German philosopher Martin Buber wrote about in his early 20th century classic *I and Thou*. This book is an example of existence as encounter. He explained this philosophy using the word pairs of "I-It" and "I–You" (or I-Thou) to denote relationships describing different modes of consciousness and interaction. Buber believed that there are two fundamental ways for us to be in the world: as subjects relating to objects (I-It) or as subjects relating to subjects (I-You). An "I-It" existence is a monologue; an individual treats other things, people, etc., as objects to be used. An "I–You" existence is a dialogue; the relationship stresses a mutual, holistic existence of two beings.

So, what is the link between empathy and *I and Thou* ? Both recognize the possibility of mutual connection at a deep level when dealing with personal and the interpersonal conflicts of our daily affairs. When our emotional capacity is stretched to the limit, when we feel vulnerable, individuals in an "I-You" relationship actively **participate** in the dynamic, living process with an "other". We seek to create a larger container to house our combustible feelings. In the same way, an empathetic individual responds with his or her whole being to the feelings and perspectives of another and uses that understanding to guide mutual actions.

The emotional and empathetic skills one brings to an "I-You" relationship can shift the consciousness between two (or more) people in mutually beneficial ways. Sometimes it may be necessary to act empathetically to achieve a desired outcome even when you feel antagonistic to a person. A psychologist who trained hostage negotiators reported the unexpected effect of "faking" empathy. Hostage negotiators are trained to act empathetically toward the hostage taker in order to establish the rapport necessary to influence him to give up and not hurt anyone. In fact, the negotiator most likely despises a person that would hold a woman and baby as hostages. What is interesting is that after a couple of hours many negotiators actually start to feel some empathy toward the hostage taker as a result of "acting" empathetic. When empathy skills are a standard part of relational interactions a higher consciousness is achieved which brings the possibilities of a more authentic relationship.

Listening to Our Inner Quiet

How do we quiet our mind enough to let the magic of empathy to unfold? One way is to listen, really listen, to another person – deeply, carefully and non-reactively. Deep listening can bring stillness into a relationship. No relationship can thrive without the sense of spaciousness that comes with stillness. But true listening is rare. Instead of listening we generally let our attention be taken up by thinking. While the other person is talking we may be evaluating his or her words preparing for our come back. Or we may not be listening at all . . . we're just lost in thought. Instead, we can go beyond the words and empathize with the other person by allowing a space of conscious presence to arise as we listen. In that space the other person is no longer "other." In that space me becomes we, joined together in one awareness, one consciousness. A moment of real attention can be enough to change the quality of the relationship. As I look and listen to the person in front of me without the prejudices of my childhood experiences and its cultural expectations, I pay attention to the stillness that surrounds both of us. That stillness – perhaps only two or three seconds of my undivided attention– is enough to go beyond the roles we play. What emerges through this act of conscious attention is my unconditioned self, my essence. This flash of shared stillness is also an acknowledgement of a simultaneous movement toward a deeper connection between us. This empathetic moment opens up a space for a more receptive realness. One plus one equals one.

Wayne's story

The setting: my office . . . or maybe an online chat. The cast of characters: two – me and my doctoral student. The purpose: jumping through seemingly impossible hoops on the path to completing a dissertation. My challenge: setting a high bar for quality work without overwhelming the student. My student's challenge: reaching that bar, in spite of all the distractions . . . the monkey mind screaming "this is too confusing," plus the endless parade of procedural hurdles that knot the stomach.

I've had the privilege of being a dissertation chair to over two dozen students. A doctoral degree is the gold standard of a discipline; it's the capstone of an academic career, a peak into generating new knowledge in the world of research and . . . it's devilishly hard work. Therein lies the dilemma. My doctoral students, mostly women between 35 – 55 years old, are high achievers. They're used to getting As. However, what worked so well in the classroom (where a syllabus described course content and grading criteria) often falls apart when they have to create their own content in an original piece of scholarship. Old demons haunt them: "Am I really up to challenge? Am I good enough to get to the finish line?" It's an unspoken fact that only half of the students who pass their Comprehensive Exams at the end of their doctoral classes actually complete their dissertation. The first real test of their mettle comes as they prepare for their proposal hearing. The cornerstone of the proposal is a defense of their hypothesis or research questions. What exactly are the variables to be measured? Their writing and thinking needs to be tight – precise and concise and clear. That task can be quite daunting; many, many drafts happen before they pass muster. In that excruciating rewrite process, they share their doubts with me. They often feel overwhelmed with a palpable sense that, at any moment, they are about to speed off a nearby cliff, one which only they can see. My job is to listen and affirm and offer a non-anxious presence. I acknowledge their feelings: "This place you are in right now is uncomfortable and disruptive. And it's OK to be right where you're at." I remind them of achieving earlier milestones, similar cliffs, which at the time also looked too steep to climb. I assure them that their bout of insecurity is a temporary madness all graduate students experience. We both take a deep breath. Slowly I become aware of my face morphing into a mischievous grin as I comment: "Say your full name out loud." Pause. "Now say it again, only this time add 'Dr.' on the front side. Go ahead now." Their body relaxes. An involuntary chuckle follows. They tentatively try on the expanded version of their soon-to-happen professional title. They sigh or shake their head in amazement. We both smile as we feel the contours of this strange place. Empathy matters.

<u>*Barb's story*</u>

When sitting with clients in a mediation setting, unexpected things happen. Although it's not often the norm, a special opening can occur when a client is able to converse in a non-confrontational way. Many clients going through a court-ordered mediation for divorce or child custody battles tend to be on high alert. Emotions run high and deep. Tempers can get out of control when parties have no way to manage or understand the magnitude of their loss. In the face of quick changes being thrust upon them they often feel as if the rug is being pulled out from underneath. Mediators have to be alert in helping clients recognize transformational possibilities during the negotiation.

During a recent session a couple came in to discuss parenting issues. However, not much progress was made due to unresolved feelings about their divorce. They were distracted. Who pulled the plug on the marriage? Fingers wagged. Judgements flew. Their deep, though invisible, wounds made it hard to negotiate the necessary pieces of the custody puzzle. Mom was talking briskly telling me what was best, in her view, for the girls. They needed solid emotional support. Her delivery was brittle and repetitive, as if she was talking to herself. Dad sat next to her, silent, seemingly a million miles away. I glanced at him and noticed tears streaming quietly down his face showing such deep sadness and fear. Mom finished her story. I turned to dad and asked what was happening for him at that moment. He poured out his heart. A wrenching sadness and overwhelming sense of loss filled the air. What was going to happen to him and his relationship to the girls? I encouraged mom to connect to that emotion as well. Hot tears flowed from of her eyes. They both looked so fragile. An emotional dam had burst. They expressed their deep sorrow for a relationship gone sideways. Yet, until that moment, neither of them had acknowledged or discussed this powerful shared feeling that had a vice grip on them. The logistics of endless paperwork and court dates, prevented them from getting at what really mattered to them. Talking about the radical change about to happen in their children's lives impacted these parents profoundly. In that raw moment, they each felt the other's pain. Empathy matters.

Chapter 4

Second Base – Grit:

Persistence in Spite of the Obstacles

"It's not that I am so smart. It's just that I stay with problems longer." Albert Einstein

"One isn't necessarily born with courage, but one is born with potential. Without courage, we cannot practice any other virtue with consistency. We can't be kind, true, merciful, generous, or honest." -Maya Angelou

A few years ago when the Lord of Rings movie trilogy was all the rage I asked a colleague to explain what all the fuss was about with Hobbits and wizards. He looked at me as if I had lost my mind. After he saw that my lack of enthusiasm made me as pitiable as Gollum, he exclaimed in an exasperated sneer, "Frodo is just an ordinary guy who steps up when he has to. That gives me hope." His identification with the hero of the story is a reminder of the power of grit to pursue a goal over a long period of time. In The Fellowship of the Ring, the first book of Tolkien's three volume set of adventures in the mythical Middle Earth, a Hobbit named Frodo begins a dangerous quest. His adventures take him to places of unimaginable beauty and terrifying anguish. He keeps on against all odds, struggles and suffers, often fails, yet perseveres nevertheless. The tale is so vivid that the reader metaphorically becomes Frodo and experiences his adventure in a deeply personal way. As Frodo discovers the internal resources to fulfill his quest, the reader can imagine tapping into his or her own inner resources to reach a personal goal despite the setbacks.

What's behind the driving force which fuels this power of grit? The key word here is "drive." Persistence and tenacity are not new concepts; nevertheless, grit is now a hot topic in psychology, business and education. What are the factors beyond normal ability which pushes someone to persevere? Angela Duckworth, a psychologist (and former school teacher) from the University of Pennsylvania, is a leading researcher on the subject of grit. She believes that "zeal" and "persistence of motive and effort" are the most crucial components of grit. In a 2007 study, she and her colleagues described grit as "perseverance and passion for long-term goals." But what does it really mean to have true grit? The most obvious answer is showing up, again and again, for a particular task, just because it is important to you. In the end, what drives success is not being exceptional but exhibiting a special blend of passion and long-term dedication toward achieving a goal. Let's look at the Instructor's Manual of how to respond when you fall down (and get up, again and again).

The WHAT of Grit

Angela Duckworth's team measured grit by looking at one's consistency of passion over time. That could be an idea percolating for a long, long time and is fueled by an incessant pursuit to bring it to fruition. Individuals who were more successful and influential than their counterparts typically possessed specific traits of enhanced effort. While ability was still critically important, these individuals also possessed "zeal" and "persistence of motive and effort." Individuals high in grit were able to maintain their determination and motivation over long periods despite failure and adversity. Their passion and commitment towards the long-term objective was the overriding factor that provided the stamina required to "stay the course" amid challenges and set-backs. Essentially, a person of strong grit saw the race as a marathon, not a sprint.

What motivates such enhanced effort? What activates the inward drive to reach your dream? The short answer: passion. In study after study of successful people in all walks of life, they identified passion and purpose as the qualities which made them successful. The Merriam-Webster dictionary defines passion as an "intense driving, or overmastering feeling or conviction." It is that drive or passion which distinguishes someone with grit. What stimulates your passion? Think for a moment of a time when you were passionate about something, when it was the sole focus of your attention, intention and action? Think about what you did to reach your goal, despite the naysayers and obstacles along the way. No doubt you followed a particular order to reach your goal. Those who have learned to focus their passion engaged in a three-step process to reach their goal: believe, accept and integrate.

1. What do you believe to achieve your dreams? For example, do you believe you are capable of planning and

implementing a plan to reach your goal? Do you believe you have enough resources (money, time, support system, etc.) to get the job done? And, ultimately, do you believe in yourself to get to the finish line?

2. Do you <u>accept</u> the conditions necessary to make this dream come true? If unanticipated changes create new conditions can you revise your expectations to get to your goal or to find your soul's calling? And, tellingly, do you have a Plan B if initial intentions or arrangements go astray?

3. Have you <u>integrated</u> the consciousness necessary for success? Are you attracting the attributes (internal fortitude, a strong desire to find the right pieces of the puzzle, the ability to pivot when necessary, etc.) to accomplish your purpose? For example, if your goal is to lose weight or develop a healthier and stronger body, are you doing something <u>every</u> <u>day</u> to make that happen? Integration means applying yourself in those areas where you have control so your effort can increase your competence.

A longer answer is about courage and resolve. What inner resources empower the strength of character necessary to get to your finish line? Character education is quite popular in public schools as a way of dealing with bullying and developing positive self-esteem. Sadly, however, most schools do not have an adequate budget to provide the curriculum (effective resources) and instruction (training and a dedicated time slot in the busy school day) to walk the talk. Good intentions are reduced to putting up inspirational slogans throughout the school building (ex: "The difference between ordinary and extraordinary is that little extra."). It's simply not enough tell students to "buck up" – to follow the command and activate internal discipline – and expect it to overcome the lifetime of unproductive habits. Rather, it's a matter of taking students where they're at, recognizing how they got there, and caring enough to invest the time and effort to help them move on. Therein lies the controversy over the effectiveness of grit.

The SO WHAT of Grit

Grit involves maintaining a goal-focused effort for extended periods of time, often while facing adversity. Folks with true grit have the self-discipline to control their impulses and pursue what they think is right despite temptations to abandon it. But impulse control does not fully account for how long people persist at something in the absence of positive feedback. To find out how top performers operated Duckworth interviewed accomplished people in various fields — sports, sales, publishing, entertainment. What distinguished high performers was largely how they processed feelings of frustration, disappointment, or boredom. When others took challenging feelings as a sign to cut their losses and turn to some easier task, high performers did not. They seemed to believe that struggle was not a signal for alarm. This key insight – change the belief about delaying when to quit and one changes the behavior about success – was the foundation of her research. Effort beats talent so success means practice, practice, practice.

Yet in our obsessively results-oriented society few people want to see the private toil of that practice. Centuries ago Michelangelo observed, "If people knew how hard I had to work to gain my mastery, it would not seem so wonderful at all." Duckworth comments that it is nearly impossible to find "effortful, mistake-ridden, repetitive deliberate practice" on YouTube. Grit may be essential. But it is not attractive." The key to routinizing this extra effort has to do with applying specific values that help people succeed. Deliberate practice is grounded in the ability to work hard toward a goal and stick to it in the face of adversity and setbacks, the resilience to rebound after failure, the inclination to do one's best even in the absence of obvious external rewards, and the willingness to delay gratification.

These nested values create conditions which can turn a perceived threat into an opportunity. Duckworth writes of growing grit from the inside out by combining perseverance and passion within a nest of Interest, Practice, Purpose and Hope. In their book Performing Under Pressure: The Science of Doing Your Best When It Matters Most, Weisinger and Pawliw-Fry identify a COTE of armor – Confidence, Optimism, Tenacity, and Enthusiasm – on how to handle pressure situations. In this book we offer the Key 3 of Empathy, Grit and Growth Mindset to meet your particular challenge which undermines success. But what happens if there is no passion nor commitment to sustain these conditions? What if the optimal conditions for grit to grow are thwarted by negative environmental factors such as poverty, social and political oppression or psychological constraints (PTSD)? What then?

Before we can look at solutions we need to understand the limits of grit. Is grit a personality trait or a learnable skill? A major implication of Duckworth's work is that grit is a skill. Schools and districts around the country are currently working hard on creating curricula and evaluation measures of grit. But, psychologists say grit isn't a skill. It's a personality trait, driven by some unknowable combination of genetics and environment. The search for a scientific way to describe personality traits goes back at least to the 1930s. But in recent decades, psychologists have settled on a group of personality dimensions known as the Big Five: conscientiousness, agreeableness, extroversion, neuroticism and openness. Many psychologists place grit as a subset of conscientiousness whose components include organization, self-control, thoughtfulness and goal-directed behavior. Herein lies the rub. Duckworth's research, grounded in education, suggests that grit is a learnable skill. Psychologists say grit is not something that's necessarily open to change, especially in adults. Even though the jury is still out on the potential of grit, the authors of this book are more interested in providing useful tools to move individuals from where they are to where they want to be.

One organization has attempted to turn those practical values into deliverables. The Rising Stars Foundation (http://risingstarsfoundation.org/) has set out to measure and build grit through their "Gritter Profile," an index to help low achievers level the playing field on their college applications. The Gritter Profile is designed to measure two things: 1) a student's ability to learn; and 2) his or her willingness to use that ability. It does not measure IQ,

Emotional Intelligence, or knowledge. The priority for them is the student's awareness of what he or she knows and what to do when he or she doesn't know. Students are measured on their ability to detect accurately their own mistakes and to seek help in understanding and correcting them" (The Rising Stars Foundation website). Gritters grit it out. They may get down when things don't go right, but being down doesn't mean being out.

That tenacity is being able to overcome limited or siloed thinking (more on that in the next chapter on growth mindset). Those who have specific strategies for dealing with unexpected disruptions can better deal with setbacks; they have an arsenal of tactics to use in challenging situations. For example, they have the ability to break down a single problem into several bite-size mini-questions that provoke thought and build critical thinking. Although grit is not tied to intelligence and is not domain-specific (that means a person may recognize and exhibit grit in a career, but not in a hobby) the gist of grit can be applied. Learning how to sustain effort over the long-term requires some time to reflect on past behaviors in order to reframe challenges or barriers to achieving a goal. That involves a different way of perceiving obstacles. What are some empowering and nonjudgmental ways to rethink or reimagine how to stay persistent?

The NOW WHAT of Grit

Do you know someone who possesses a dogged determination to succeed? Perhaps it's someone fighting the battle for an unpopular cause or someone who endures one rejection letter after another before finally getting a "right-fit" job or seeing one's book published. What kept them going? If you could get inside this person's head, you might get a clue to how their thinking propels such persistent behavior? How do they translate good intentions into appropriate choices? An excellent book has been written on how to free ourselves from the conditioned responses of our past: The Ten Commitments: Translating Good Intentions into Great Choices by Dr. David Simon. The premise of the book is to turn away from a "commandment" mentality to a "commitment" mindset. For example, the commandment Moses gave against graven images is transformed into a personal commitment to authenticity; the commandment to observe the Sabbath becomes a commitment to relax.

The shift from a commandment mindset to a commitment mindset gets at the heart of what causes limiting beliefs. Most people believe that the cause of their unhappiness come from external forces: "I'm depressed because I am in a loveless marriage," or "I am getting an ulcer due to an overbearing boss." However, if you dig a bit deeper you'll find some semi-conscious internal voices suffocating your creativity, enthusiasm and joy. How can we release those restrictive demons? Dr. Simon, a neurologist, now associated with The Chopra Center, offers two insights that can expand your perception of Self. The first is to commit your whole self to action. When you make a commitment, you dedicate the entirety of your ABCs to the task: you align your observing heart (Affective) and acknowledge the accumulation of small steps of progress (Behavioral) and practice a concentrated focus of mind (Cognitive). When these parts are lined up together, you are more likely to translate your intentions into choices that result in the desired outcome. The second insight is to favor commitment over affirmation. Although affirmation is important for emotional support and encouragement, it has its limits. Constantly affirming something seldom leads to lasting change. Successful people do not say over and over, "I am a powerful person." Instead they ask, "What do I really want? Am I prepared to take the steps to get it?" When you make a commitment, you dedicate yourself to a course of action that you believe will result in the expansion of happiness and wellbeing. Your cognitive mindset reflects the person you really want to be. The person who wants to be happy and attract meaning and purpose in life hears and understands the quiet voices of your soul calling.

Equally as important, how does one translate that understanding into productive action? How do we stay consistent in reaching our goal, especially since we have past habits that have caused excess swerving? In short, how can we balance flexibility and grit? These questions do not have one simple answer. Grit is needed to provide direction to get somewhere and it can also provide a compass if we are forced to switch paths. We need grit to get past hard-to-give-up habits. We create these new practices when we embrace (rather than fight or run from) the tensions of our intentions. We recommend some form of meditation to release the mental or emotional strain preventing deep change. A study at the University of Oregon found that meditating for 30 minutes five days a week helped students regulate thoughts and behaviors and emotions more effectively. Meditation formats vary. It can be stationary (sitting or standing or lying down) or moving (tai chi), focusing on breath or focusing on a sound or an object. The key is to include three components: relaxation, mental imagery and mindfulness. Ultimately meditation helps resolve deeply personal conundrums of knowing when to adapt or when to persist, when to risk or when to trust. And, most beneficially, the effects of meditation can help you detach from being too self-conscious to being conscious of your larger potential.

Listening to Our Inner Quiet

The inner voice of the soul finds expression when you can allow a consciousness of abundance to blossom. One way it begins is to believe you have a wealthy imagination. However, to trigger the potential of an unbridled imagination you have to give something up. This means more than simply giving up a pleasure as many do during the Lenten season. It's more fundamental than that. This letting go, this empowered action, is oh-so-simple to state, yet oh-so-difficult to achieve. What's the magic potion? A three word answer: accept what *is*. Accepting what *is* takes you to a deeper place where your inner state no longer depends of the mind's judgments of "good" or "bad." Accepting what *is* means surrendering to this moment and not the story through which you interpret this moment (and then following a second-best path with reluctance or resignation). Accepting what *is* means not labeling this moment. Does this mean being happy with a dysfunctional situation? Nope. It means letting phenomenon arise, then letting it go so you can respond to the next helping on your plate. For example, if an auto accident has paralyzed your legs, you would probably feel despair. It would be understandable if you saw yourself as a victim and reacted, "Why is this happening to me?" A more proactive response would be to acknowledge the moment and move on. Someone accepting the *what is* of this moment might say, "I will be needing a wheelchair to get around." The condition is as it is. Without the compulsion to argue for the rightness or wrongness of a situation or person or place, this present moment can be filled with an alert stillness. This state of inner nonresistance permits something new to bubble up – an unconditioned consciousness. This mental state is infinitely larger than the human mind. Here is the wellspring of the imagination.

Sigh! You may be thinking "Great on paper but how can I get from imaginative thoughts to tangible results?" Truth be told, a genuine metamorphosis in your thinking will involve a dramatic transformation in consciousness. In physics the spontaneous change by a nuclear process of one element into another is called a transformation. For example, think of the change of water from a solid to a liquid to a gas. Remember, this change process does not happen without a transfer of energy. Likewise, your personal transformation will require a transfer of energy on your part. In our experience, the use of queries can stimulate that transfer of energy. A transformative change of your values, beliefs and aspirations starts with questioning your assumptions about change. Reflect on what you can do, <u>right now</u>, to create a more viable path. Think of what you want to change in your life, what you want to get rid of or what you want to attract. Then use these queries to clarify how you will proceed with your transformation. Be honest with yourself. Be willing to transfer fresh energy into a new way of knowing. And, of course, be kind to yourself during the process of change.

- What do I need to change in my life to allow my commitment to blossom?

- What is it costing me if I do not continue to change?

- What is it costing others close to me if I do not continue to change?

- Am I empowering others or enabling others with my unproductive choices?

- What will it cost me one year from now if I don't make the shift? (What will it cost me 5 years from now?)

- What baby steps can I take <u>right now</u> to fulfill my desires?

- What are the benefits for me (and for others) with a shift to a new commitment?

- Does the shift to a new commitment bring me a happier life?

<u>Wayne's story</u>

My mid-life crisis was brought on by a perfect storm of too much work, not enough play and a whole lot of loneliness. The years leading to my fall were a whirlwind: working on my doctorate, teaching undergraduate intro classes on penury wages, straining to fulfill my parental obligations and subsisting on a lifestyle high on caffeine and low on sleep. It's no wonder that my first marriage imploded. I thought, erroneously, that I would right the balance when I landed a tenure-line position at a respected university. Nope, the dangling knife of "publish or perish" expectations kept me on the academic conveyer belt 24/7. In my mind, I was not worried. I always had a lot of energy and a strong physical constitution. I could do anything I put my mind to. I could meet any challenge. Then . . . BAM! The attitude of invincibility clouded my judgment and ultimately took me down. My push-push life style was acid to my immune system. I was totally unprepared for the knockout punch. The fatigue, which I attributed to overwork and the effects of a lingering cold, were, in fact, symptoms of Crohn's Disease, an extremely painful inflammation of the digestive tract. My body collapsed. I couldn't eat solid foods. My well-planned life was in shambles. And my magnificent willpower, which had saved me from previous calamities, went AWOL. The old formulas of success no longer worked. I lost a third of my body weight. I lost one hundred percent of my confidence. I was desperate enough to pray. And that prayer was utterly simple. God, show me the way. Happily, I was shown a way: seven abdominal surgeries in five years, a complete remake of my diet, daily meditation and reducing stress by allowing gratitude to replace judgments. The necessary changes did not come easily. I am a stubborn guy. I yearned for the comforts of my old life. They never came. What did come, however was the bounty of my present life. I set new goals. I failed. I learned from my mistakes and kept on steppin'. Grit matters.

Barb's story

Pursuing a doctorate most certainly qualifies as an extreme sport. There are research classes to take, a Comp Exam to survive (the mother of all tests on everything you know) and, of course, that little project called the dissertation. It was a rollercoaster of emotions. One moment, I was excited and energized about advancing knowledge. However, that mood quickly dissipated when I tried to write in a scholarly fashion following accepted research protocols. No, no, there were WAY too many moving parts! And how does one share such a complicated project with family or friends? To help me get clarity about my topic my committee chair schooled me on the "elevator speech." It goes like this: a colleague you haven't seen in ages gets on the elevator, sees you and asks, "How's your research going? What's your dissertation about?" You have only enough time – two or three floors, at best – to unravel your spiel. Sheesh. If that's not impossible, what is? The writing standards are exacting. One needs to be clear, precise and concise but, for me, this does not qualify as natural behavior. Critical thinking and creativity has to be woven throughout each of the chapters. And the reward for my labors? I get an opportunity to "defend" my dissertation, a two-hour presentation and grilling by my committee. Invariably they asked a few questions (it seemed like a gazillion) that totally stumped me. So much for being the expert. After I passed (survived is more like it) I could reflect. What did the process teach me? My answer – you reach, then reach some more, then just when you think you are done reaching, you have to reach a bit further still.

Each dissertation is unique but every grad student has a tale of an unexpected disaster, an incident that is beyond the pale. For me it involved a last second switch-a-roo. After I defended my dissertation, revised it, and hired a copy editor to cross T's and dot I's to make it scholarship worthy, I turned in my precious document to the Dean. The Dean initially signed off but then reconsidered. More "reach" was needed. This side trajectory blindsided me and my committee. What followed was an academic circus to get everyone on the same page. You've no doubt, heard the expression "politics can play so rough." To say I was a stressed-out crazy woman doesn't even come close to what was actually going on in my head. Did I feel like giving up? Are you kidding? Every day! But something inside me, an insistent voice, kept up this mantra: "I earned this. I've worked hard for this, I will prevail." Throughout the entire process, my team stood by me; their grit was palpable. Finally, after oh-so-many revisions and tears, the masterpiece was deemed acceptable and I got that coveted signature. Whew! A weight lifted off my shoulders. I was SO tired but I had realized my goal. Grit matters.

Chapter 5

Third Base – Growth Mindset:

Facing Challenges By Learning From Our Mistakes

"When people are ready to, they change. They never do it before then, and sometimes they die before they get around to it. You can't make them change if they don't want to, just like when they do want to, you can't stop them." Andy Warhol

"That he not busy being born is busy dying." Bob Dylan

My [WB] first real job after college was teaching in an inner-city elementary school. My students were categorized as low-income: they lived in a federal housing project surrounding the school; over 90% were on free or reduced lunches. Most kids came from single-parent homes. Full-time work was scarce. The two nearby employers, a distillery and a rendering plant, paid decent wages but offered no real job security; national companies were off-shoring manufacturing jobs to cut labor costs. Families were transient, constantly on the lookout for cheap or safe housing. It would not be uncommon to see the same student on my class roster three separate times in a school year. During the warm months, the scent of marijuana drifted into our classroom window as teenagers openly smoked joints on the asphalt playground which doubled as a public park. Several of my students, even as early as second grade, were victims of random violence. My colleagues and I experienced an impossibly huge disconnect between what was being taught in my teacher preparation classes and the chaos in my students' homes and neighborhood. My professional goal was to create lessons to help them thrive. However, their main focus was simply to survive. Nevertheless, by the end of my two year Teacher Corps commitment, I realized how much we needed each other. From me, they learned how to think critically, engage collaboratively and respect diverse opinions and beliefs. From them, I learned that real learning wasn't going to happen unless it was relevant to their life and it was fun.

Schools track academic progress through annual standardized testing. Ideally, the schools adequate yearly progress, or AYP, of a student would be one year of academic gain in a nine-month school year. My incoming fourth graders should have been at the 3.9 or 4.0 level when we started the school year. However, their average reading scores was 2.6; their math score was even lower, 1.9. That meant they were a year-and-a-half behind in reading and two years behind in math from their grade peers in national averages . . . and they were only a quarter of the way through their 12-year formal schooling. Expectations were low. My principal told us to aim at reducing annual academic loss by half (i.e. they would lose only 2 – 3 months per year rather than 5 in reading and 3 – 4 months rather than 7 in math). My student's parents were more practical: "Just keep them out of trouble and keep them in school. I can't afford to take off work for any foolishness." Yet my expectations (and those of my Teacher Corps buddies) were far higher. If given the right resources and support why couldn't they make a full year's progress in one academic year? That was our charge. We did all sorts of wild and crazy things, from experimenting with new instructional strategies (like small group discussion groups) to conducting "real world" research out in the community (like price comparisons for bread and milk from the same grocery chain a suburban store versus one inner city store). At first our students were mistrustful of our motives but they eventually came to see that they "owned" their learning. School had become meaningful for them. Their academic scores skyrocketed. If they followed the pace from previous years, the end-of-the-year reading scores would have advanced from 2.6 to 3.1; the principal was shooting for a range of 3.3 or 3.4; I was hoping their average score would be 3.6. My kid's test scores surprised even me: They jumped from 2.6 to and 4.1, a year-and-a-half academic gain in nine months . . . from a rookie teacher. What did I do to make this happen? I got them to believe that they could become who they wanted to be and accomplish the things they value. In short, I got them to move from fixed mindset to growth mindset.

The WHAT of Growth Mindset

Why do some kids succeed in school and others fail, even when they come from the same neighborhood or home? Educational policy and practice during the last 25 years to close the achievement gap between low- and high- income students has been a total bust. Again, why? The takeaway from the last chapter was this – we need grit to get past hard-to-give-up habits. Yet according to Camille A. Farrington, a former inner-city high school teacher who works at the University of Chicago Consortium on School Research, "There is little evidence that working directly on changing students' grit or perseverance would be an effective lever for improving their academic performance. While some students are more likely to persist in tasks or exhibit self-discipline in others, *all* students are more likely to demonstrate perseverance if the school or classroom context helps them develop positive mindsets and effective learning strategies." Her team discovered that a student's academic perseverance – how they maintained positive academic performance despite setbacks – depends on his or her academic mindset. Those students with a positive academic mindset had more resilience based on four key beliefs:

1. I belong in this academic community;
2. My ability and competence grow with my effort;
3. I succeed at this;
4. This work has value for me.

Students holding these beliefs in mind were more likely to persist through challenging academic work and not give up when their initial efforts failed. What explains this?

Two decades of research by Carol S. Dweck, a psychologist at Stanford, have shown the enormous impact teachers have on a student's mindset. Her studies distinguish between two categories of behavior based on a student's reaction to failure, a fixed mindset or a growth mindset. Dweck claims that those with a fixed mindset believe that intelligence is static which leads to a desire to look smart and avoid challenges which might endanger that image. When obstacles occur, they give up easily; effort is seen as fruitless. Therefore, they ignore useful feedback if it is negative and feel threatened by the success of others. As a result they may plateau early and achieve less than their full potential, confirming their deterministic view of the world. On the other hand, students with a growth mindset believe that intelligence can be developed which leads to a desire to embrace challenges so they can learn more. They see effort as a path to mastery and persist in the face of setbacks. Therefore, they learn from criticism and find lessons and inspiration in the success of others. As a result they reach higher levels of achievement which gives them a greater sense of free will.

In multiple studies, Carol Dweck and her colleagues noted that alterations in mindset could be achieved through praising the effort which led to success. Effective praise was not general ("Great effort. You tried your best.") but specific and contextual ("A good first try. This is new information for you. Learning happens in stages. The point is to grow into the next step. What are you going to try next?"). Such focused praise impacts a student's achievement motivation by satisfying their internal and external need for success. Dweck's research of mindsets has been useful in intervention strategies with at-risk students, dispelling negative stereotypes in education held by teachers and students, especially through an understanding of how process praise can foster a growth mindset. Individuals who believe their talents can be developed (through hard work, good strategies, and input from others) have a growth mindset. They tend to achieve more than those with a more fixed mindset (those who believe their talents are innate gifts). This is because they worry less about looking smart and they put more energy into learning.

Business reframed these concepts to productive (or abundance) mindset versus the defensive (or scarcity) mindset. The productive reasoning mindset creates conditions for informed choices and makes reasoning transparent which encourages the effort to seek valid knowledge that is testable. The defensive mindset, on the other hand, can be self-deceptive. When this mindset is active, people or organizations only seek out information that will protect them. Truth can be shut out when it is seen as threatening. When entire companies embrace a growth mindset, their employees report feeling far more empowered and committed; they also receive far greater organizational support for collaboration and innovation. In contrast, people at primarily fixed-mindset companies report more of only one thing: cheating and deception among employees, presumably to gain an advantage in the talent race.

This illustrates the key difference between the two mindsets — for those with a growth mindset, personal success means working your hardest to become your best. For those with fixed mindset success means establishing your superiority; the bottom line for them is that it is better to show others that you are a somebody, not a nobody. One of the most profound applications of this insight has less to do with education or business but with love. Dweck found that people exhibited the same reactions in their personal relationships. Those with a fixed mindset believed their ideal mate would put them on a pedestal and make them feel perfect, whereas those with the growth mindset preferred a partner who would recognize their faults and lovingly help improve them. In the fixed mindset, the ideal is effortless and perpetual compatibility; cue to the end of a romantic movie: as the credits roll on the screen the implication is that the couple "lives happily ever". The growth mindset, however, says that you, your partner, and the relationship are capable of growth and change. The motivation in the relationship is to encourage your partner to learn new things and became a better person.

All relationships have conflict. It's interesting to note how mindsets affect our response to disagreements. When people with a fixed mindset talk about their conflicts, they assign blame. Sometimes they blame themselves, but often they blame their partner. Making matters worse they claim that the responsibility for a fault or wrong is based on a personality trait, a character flaw. A predictable defensive reaction results. Since the problem comes from fixed traits, it can't be solved. So once people with the fixed mindset see flaws in their partners, they become angry and disgusted with them and dissatisfied with the whole relationship. However, those with the growth mindset can acknowledge their partners' imperfections without assigning blame, and still feel that they have a fulfilling relationship. Conflicts are seen as problems of communication, not of personality or character. The irony is obvious. We begin a relationship with a partner who is different from us – it's the source of our attraction -and then become offended when those same differences erupt in conflict. In a healthy relationship people develop skills to deal with their differences. As they do, their relationship deepens. But for this to happen, people need to feel they're on the same side, the side of growth as an individual and as a couple. Success comes when we do our best to allow "us" to grow. Yes, supporting uncomfortable changes in the relationship, allowing both "me" and "we" to grow, can be incredibly difficult, full of obstacles, and we know we're going to make it. This unshakeable validation of each other's development helps create an atmosphere of trust. A relationship-based growth mindset thrives on challenge and sees failure as a heartening springboard for stretching our existing abilities. There is no perceived deficit. No need to prove our worth. Just the effort to get better, individually and together.

What it all comes down to is this: a mindset is an interpretative process that tells us what is going on around us. In the fixed mindset, that process is underscored by an internal monologue of constant judging and evaluation. Do I (or he or she or they) measure up? In a growth mindset, on the other hand, the internal monologue is not one of judgment but one of voracious appetite for learning, constantly seeking out the kind of input that leads to understanding and constructive action.

The SO WHAT of Growth Mindset

Why is growth mindset such a hot topic right now? We get a hint from evolutionary psychology. This field **attempts to explain mental and psychological traits, such as memory,**

perception, or language, as adaptations. Research suggests that humans evolved social characteristics because group behavior helped them survive. Mindset studies can provide a context to explain human adaptation to changing environments, specifically what is useful to produce more effective workplaces and classrooms. If an employee or student believed their qualities were carved in stone, **the fixed mindset,** there would be an urgency to prove yourself over and over. If you felt limited in intelligence or personality or moral character you'd have a strong incentive to avoid looking deficient in these most basic characteristics. Every situation calls for a confirmation of your intelligence, personality, or character, all fueled by a keen desire to avoid feeling stupid or being perceived as a loser. Someone with a fixed mindset wants to look smart and will give up chances to face more challenging work for fear of making mistakes or failing. Setbacks are not handled well since they feel like their intelligence is being challenged. They can easily become defensive or discouraged often quit what they are working on, blame others for the inability to complete a task, lie, and even cheat to show themselves as smart.

There's another mindset where the hand you're dealt is just the starting point for development. This ***growth mindset*** is based on the belief that your basic qualities are things you can cultivate through your efforts. Although people may differ in their talents interests, or temperaments, there is a fundamental belief that everyone can change and grow through application and experience. Students who believe that intelligence can be grown and nurtured welcome challenges. Even young children experiencing moments of successful learning by conquering obstacles use these experiences as evidence that they can influence their outcomes. A growth mindset prepares students for success through even the hardest of challenges because the effort is appreciated and desired. Not being able to complete something is not viewed as a failure but as an opportunity for growth. They believe their curiosity about new ideas and perspectives will help them solve future problems. Intuitively they understand that even geniuses work hard.

When a person with a growth mindset faces a new challenge, they take it on with the fascination of rising to a new level by expanding their repertoire of knowledge and skills. Three behaviors shine with growth-mindset individuals:

1. They are <u>open to changing their mind</u> when presented with compelling evidence. For example, in one study of a cognitive simulation which posed an anomaly or new information, growth-mindset people were more likely to change their initial understanding of a situation over previous beliefs.

2. They are hungry for <u>feedback</u>, positive or negative, as a means for growth. This frees them up considerably. They can risk making a mistake because they might find new strategies and behaviors to solve a problem.

3. They are more apt to use reflection as a way to gain <u>fresh perspective</u>. Unlike a fixed mindset person who sees reflection as extra effort, growth mindset people see reflection as part of the process of being a deliberate learner.

However, a note of caution needs to be given. Eager to jump on this provocative bandwagon, many people jump to false conclusions about growth mindset. Dweck identifies three common misconceptions of a false growth mindset where the basic understanding of the idea is limited:

1. Always had it, always will – People often confuse a growth mindset with being flexible or open-minded or with having a positive outlook. However, everyone is actually a mixture of fixed and growth mindsets, and that mixture continually evolves with experience. A "pure" growth mindset doesn't exist. We have to recognize that if we really want to grow.

2. Praise matters more than outcomes – Nope, unproductive effort is never a good thing. It's important to honor both learning and progress, and to emphasize the processes that yield these things. Outcomes are met when deeply engaged processes are followed, such as seeking help from others, trying new strategies, and capitalizing on setbacks to move forward.

3. Talk the talk and good things will happen – Another nope. Slogans on the classroom wall or mission statements with lofty values about growth are not enough. Cultures supporting growth mindset, not just in words but in deeds, encourage appropriate risk-taking, knowing that some risks won't work out. They reward students or employees for important and useful lessons learned, even if a project does not meet its original goals.

However, even correcting these misconceptions does not guarantee reaching a growth mindset. We still have to deal with our own fixed-mindset triggers. When we face challenges, receive criticism, or do poorly compared with others, we can easily fall prey to insecurity or defensiveness, a response that inhibits growth. Also, we need to recognize institutional barriers to a growth mindset. The classroom or office can be full of fixed-mindset triggers that impede growth such as sharing information, collaborating, innovating, seeking feedback, or admitting errors. To remain in a growth zone, we must identify and work with these triggers. It takes courage to put growth mindset processes into practice. What constructive thoughts, words and behaviors will you use when your fixed-mindset demon shows up? What can we do to model these practices of a deeper, more engaged growth mindset?

The NOW WHAT of Growth Mindset

The growth mindset can be developed if given the proper guidance. Attitude and perspective about a new task makes all the difference. A teacher who can present something challenging as fun and exciting will have a better chance at nurturing the growth mindset. Coming at a task as if it is a mystery to be solved allows those frustrated students to see this as a positive moment, not one to be feared. The teacher who wants to encourage a growth mindset in a student knows how to point out when targeted effort can improve performance. Understanding the benefits of allowing students to struggle, and even fail from time-to-time, can motivate them to recover from failures. Learning flexible and effective problem-solving strategies can relieve the stress of the moment.

However, Dweck and her colleagues are finding an unsettling disconnect between the talk and walk of growth mindset. During workshops and presentations around the country she hears stories from many teachers and parents who endorse growth mindset rhetoric but react to children's mistakes in ways that unintentionally promote fixed mindset practice. For example, reiterating the message "just try harder" can backfire. Most students have heard "just try harder," ad nauseum but they also need to understand why they should put in effort and how to deploy that effort. Compare these two statements:

1. *"Don't worry, you'll get it if you keep trying."*

2. *"That problem is hard. I've seen you do hard things before. What can you try now that'll help you solve this problem?"*

The first statement is feel-good cheerleading. The second statement uses the student's past success as evidence to bolster her current effort. Responding with growth mindset thinking will require us to relearn how we deal with challenges. Dweck's remedy to match the words and actions of growth mindset is to pay attention to our fixed-mindset triggers:

> *Watch for a fixed-mindset reaction when you face challenges. Do you feel overly anxious, or does a voice in your head warn you away? Watch for it when you face a setback in your teaching, or when*

students aren't listening or learning. Do you feel incompetent or defeated? Do you look for an excuse? Watch to see whether criticism brings out your fixed mindset. Do you become defensive, angry, or crushed instead of interested in learning from the feedback? Watch what happens when you see an educator who's better than you at something you value. Do you feel envious and threatened, or do you feel eager to learn? Accept those thoughts and feelings and work with and through them. And keep working with and through them. (Dweck, Carol, *Mindset: The New Psychology of Success*)

It takes a lot of work and a lot of time for this reorientation to feel natural. We must avoid the temptation to oversimplify: growth mindset means you are an enlightened person and fixed mindset means you are an unenlightened person. We have seen teachers and office workers immediately claim a growth mindset identity after just one workshop. How can we break through this false mindset thinking? Again, Dweck to the rescue. She urges us to use a dual voice (both/and) response. We're all a mixture of fixed and growth mindsets. The key is to practice, again and again, these essential mindset principles:

- Intelligence can be developed
- The brain is malleable
- Doing challenging work is the best way to make the brain stronger and smarter

If we watch carefully for our fixed-mindset triggers, we can begin the true journey to a growth mindset.

Mindsets can be changed, but most American schools don't do a good job of creating environments that develop positive mindsets and effective learning strategies. Some teachers have been able to create such an environment in their own classroom regardless of the school climate, however schoolwide strategies promoting growth mindset have been rare. Paul Tough, the author of the best-selling book How Children Succeed, has documented several schools that help students become more resilient. The "Turnaround for Children," a school transformation network (nonprofit), with schools in New York, Newark, New Jersey and Washington DC, coaches teachers to provide a more inviting emotional atmosphere by creating a climate of belonging and engagement in the classroom. Students can follow the muse of their curiosity when a variety of instructional strategies are employed, such as cooperative learning, small group peer review and collaborative long-term projects. The EL (Expeditionary Learning) Education, a national nonprofit network of 150 schools throughout the country, has a particular emphasis on high poverty schools. EL education successfully uses two strategies to develop an ongoing academic mindset in its students. The first strategy deals with belonging and relationship and the second immerses students in challenging academic work. Classrooms in both systems are designed to be more engaging and interactive than classrooms in most American schools. Students feel more motivated when they experience deep and close relationships and do work that is challenging, rigorous and meaningful.

However, such schools are rare. Teachers and parents who are drawn to such empowering environments of education can find comprehensive strategies through the online Khan Academy growth mindset lesson plan

[https://s3.amazonaws.com/KA-share/Toolkit-photos/FINAL%20Growth%20Mindset%20Lesson%20Plan%20(April%202015).pdf].

Here's a sample of the type of activities in this free pdf:

- As a teacher, share a personal story about a time you had to work hard to get better at something and relate it to the video. In this story, highlight:

  1. Hard work
  2. Strategies
  3. Help from others

- Ask your students for a short story about a struggle they had when they were learning. How did it make them feel? How did they overcome it, and what did it teach them? Tell them to write a letter to a future student to tell them about their struggle, what they learned from it, and any advice they could give for the student

- Have students do a research project on how the brain grows as it struggles to learn something new. Ask students to create a poster, diorama, painting, video, or PowerPoint presentation to showcase how the brain works. Also be sure that students include evidence to back up their claims Encourage students to be creative and scientific when explaining how learning can help develop the brain.

They may choose from the options listed:

- What is neuroplasticity and how does it work?
- What are neurons? How can they change over time? How do we know this?
- What are ways of making your brain grow?
- What is a growth mindset?

The consequences of believing that intelligence and personality can be developed rather than being immutably engrained traits, can profoundly affect your life. The view you take for yourself can determine whether you become the person you want to be, that is, the person who can accomplish what's important to you. How? What interior changes move you forward to growth mindset?

Listening to Our Inner Quiet

A fixed mindset causes us to believe that we are not entitled to life's bounty. This robs us of our sense of awe and wonder. William Blake's captures this sensibility by reminding us to "kiss the joy as it flies." On the other hand, when we are consciously connected to creating the reality of our dreams, a feeling of appreciation arises. It makes sense. Why wouldn't we be thankful after we give ourselves permission to let our heart's desire open us up?

Surrendering to our heart, not our head, creates optimal conditions to be happier and more balanced. A growth mindset increases in proportion to our ability to see what's good in life. This potential gets fed when we are grateful. By not taking life for granted we become grateful for everything life offers (regardless of our mind's interpretation of what's good, bad or ugly), especially with what comes up unexpectedly. When we can be more open and accepting and vulnerable to whatever feeling is on our plate gratitude blossoms naturally. The 20th century German poet, Rainer Maria Rilke, underscored this fluidity of life: "Let everything happen to you: beauty and terror. / Just keep going. No feeling is final." Now take a step back and personalize this attitude. Think of a time in your life when you showed sincere appreciation for the "beauty and terror" of your fate. Perhaps it was a threatening situation that needed to be assimilated. Perhaps it was a pushback on a robotic internal monologue which is eroding your self-worth. Use these queries to let the light of gratitude shine on the shadows surrounding unfinished business you want to make in your life. Give yourself permission to count your blessings.

- What do I take for granted?
- What relationships in my life do I cherish (people, pets, etc.)
- What unique gifts or opportunities do I have?
- What advantages or freedoms have I been given in life?
- Who is my support crew, the champions in my life?

Finally, meditate on this snippet by Joseph Campbell, who brought fresh wisdom to old myths: "The demon that you can swallow gives you its power, and the greater life's pain, the greater life's reply."

Wayne's story

This may seem frivolous but my change from fixed mindset to growth mindset involved dancing with my wife. Actually, it's more basic than that. I was terrified about being on a dance floor. I knew, without hesitation, that everybody was looking only at me and wincing at my uncoordinated gyrations. Although I felt good about my body image and enjoyed playing several sports when it came to cutting the rug, I could only let out my inner clunk. I did my due diligence in trying to learn new dance moves (in the privacy of my home, of course). I studied film, mostly of Fred Astaire and Gene Kelly. I imagined I was a gazelle. But, in reality, I knew who I was – a heavy hippo. As fate would have it I married a woman who really loved to dance. Her movements were quite graceful too. She simply glided around the dance floor as if she was an Olympic ice skater. When we were courting she tried everything to get me to move rhythmically. "Just relax," she'd coo, "and let your body follow the beat of music." I heard her words but they did not compute physically. My body felt like a brick. I was a hopeless case. Until the day she accidently unlocked the combination to my winged feet. The timing and setting were so unexpected. We were packing for a move. Boxes, some packed, most not, cluttered our living room. We were hot and tired. One of our favorite songs came on the radio. She took my hand and spontaneously spun me around in a little pirouette. I have no memory what happened after that. We swayed, we whirled, we twirled. The song ended but we continued to dance. Finally we collapsed in a heap on the couch. "She shook her head from side to side and asked, "What just happened?" I shrugged my shoulders and said "I dunno, but that was fun, wasn't it?" Truth be told, I dropped my need to hide behind my perceived deficiency and just let the passion of the moment overtake me. That moment was a real deal changer. I realized I could put new wine in old skins. I wanted to recreate this moment again. Happily, my wife and I have had numerous opportunities for "deliberate practice." I know I am not the most elegant guy on the dance floor, but I have fun stretching myself and now look forward to dancing with my wife. Growth mindset matters.

Barb's story

Sometimes new ways of thinking come out of unexpected places. Making life decisions has always been challenging for me. I am the type of person who has to know all of the options and then I think through each of the details – the implications, consequences and fantasies – of why one choice is better than another. And, heaven forbid, I don't let anyone know how much obsessing I do! It's an exhausting process. Sometimes this constant self-questioning simply paralyzes me.

Here's a for instance. A while back, a coveted job offer, complete with two separate trainings, was dumped in my lap. Naturally I was excited . . . until I saw the dates of the trainings. The multi day trainings came at the same time as a dear friend's wedding and another "must do" event which had been scheduled 7 months earlier. What to do? What to do? Before, I would have fretted privately. This time I did something new. I called up a friend and fretted with him. I talked and talked and talked about the implications, consequences and fantasies of the decision until I had nothing left to say. At the end of our conversation, two things became apparent to me: the decision needed to came more from my heart than my head and speaking my truth was really, really important. When I truly listened to myself I "knew" that my heart was at peace. I had a resolution: I would be available for the first training and I would need to miss the second training. I notified the firm. The ball regarding next steps was now in their court. I felt relieved and would accept whatever outcome happened.

Indeed, this was a growth mindset for me. My natural inclination was a fixed response, to please others first before attending to my own needs. Having that conversation with a friend when I was most vulnerable was a huge step for me. I was able to compare two different assessments of the situation and I was affirmed for sharing the rumblings of my heart. Growth mindset matters.

Chapter 6

Getting to Home Plate: Living With Our Questions

"Live your questions now, and perhaps even without knowing it, you will live along some distant day into your answers." Rainer Maria Rilke

A thought exercise. Draw a horizontal line on a paper, 12 inches in length. Now extend the line 3 inches on each side with dotted lines. The right end of the line represents your fluid life, your abundant life, your life as you choose it in the present moment from an I/Thou perspective. The left end of the line represents your fixed life with a focus on deficits and limitations, a life of indecision fixated on the past or future. These are symptoms of an I/It perspective. The solid line is what you already know; the dotted lines are what's unknown, what experiences and people you are attracting. Now place a fulcrum somewhere along the solid horizontal line as a graphic representation of how you view your life unfolding. Be as honest and nonjudgmental as you can. If the fulcrum is not at the midpoint of the horizontal line (a rare event for most of us) and you are eager to find a rough balance, pay attention to the dotted lines. The fulcrum is a stationary point. The weight and length of the line are the variables you can control to get balance. An image from my childhood tells the tale. As a teenager I remember hoisting my five-year-old sister permanently into the up position by sitting down on my end of the seesaw. If she had more weight on her side or if I moved closer to the center (or a combination of the two) the teeter totter would be in perfect balance. Same with your needs and aspirations as you strive to live into your fullness. What are you going to move (surrender) on the left side of the line or give weight to (intentionality) on the right side of the line to put your line in a rough balance? What questions do you need to ask yourself to move toward that balance?

This chapter is about applying any combination of the Key 3 (empathy, grit or growth mindset) to your particular hot-button issue. It answers the question: How do I claim my light to get unstuck from negative beliefs and follow my calling? First though, a digression on the art of questioning. Effective questioning is the lifeblood of a teacher or a counselor or a mediator. Questioning taps into the art of learning and is WAY more important than the rush to spit out a "correct" answer. Despite what your teachers may have told you, there IS such a thing as a bad question. A bad question forces a learner to get into the mind of the teacher and make a knee-jerk guess. This response to a question is focused on pleasing the question-asker; as a result, students often internalize straitjacketed thinking and shallow recall which summons an anxiety to perform. A good question, on the other hand, forces the learner to make a deep dive into his or her mind. The response to a good question encourages independent and original thinking; students are rewarded for curiosity and risk-taking. A student or client answering a good question takes into account the context (the complexity of the circumstance and competing perceptions on how to respond) of the question and the metacognition (the awareness and understanding of one's own thought processes) of the question-answerer.

Which brings us back to you. In the first chapter we proposed an educational model to help make your dreams come true. We suggested the Key 3 principles of empathy, grit and growth mindset to reframe the story of who you say you are. In this chapter we get personal.

> *Are you willing to ask yourself the tough questions to increase your learning capacity?*

> *Are you willing (at least in your mind's eye) to be open-minded and open-hearted on the journey to a more competent and confident you?*

> *Finally, are you willing to be more accountable in making and maintaining sustainable changes, <u>even after you initially fall down</u>?*

If you answered "yes" then you are ready to live your questions now. Use the questions posed in this chapter to grapple with your issue – overcoming negativity or dissolving the barriers to your calling – to trust your instincts to follow new hunches. Embrace these questions as much as you can, especially the scary ones.

The WHAT of questioning

Effective questions are questions that are thought-provoking. The most effective questions are less concerned with an immediate (and often superficial) answer but in what new questions it raises. They are not "why" questions, but "what" and "how" questions. "Why" questions can lead us to reinforce set beliefs instead of disrupting set beliefs. Rather than soliciting a fresh point of view, "why" questions can scratch insecurities and make people defensive. Instead, ask more powerful questions about what's going on and how conditions might be changed.

Effective questions linger. The kind of questions we ask lead us to the kind of answers we seek. We can ask closed questions or open questions. Closed questions give a narrow focus and can be helpful when checking facts, clarifying a point or providing some direction on the topic at hand. These are usually beginning questions that give boundaries to an issue. Open questions provide more breadth and depth and can be helpful to gaining more detailed information, exploring ideas and clarifying thoughts. These are usually the follow-up questions that give context to an issue. Consider some of these questions as you work with your particular issue. Frame your issue as a question. Start with easy questions and progress to more challenging ones.

> *What causes me to abandon my effort after a disappointment (ex: losing weight, eating right, exercising, making more money, finding a right-fit job, finding a compatible partner, etc.)?*

> *How does this situation mirror an aspect of myself?*

> *What are my old mental messages or beliefs about this?*

> *What tools will help me with this situation?*

Effective questions follow effective listening. When asking effective questions, it is important to listen mindfully to get to a deeper level of understanding. Listening in this manner allows the student or client to come up with their own solution or plan of action. To do so, consciously move from low-level listening where the attention is on me (thinking of your response as he or she talks to you) to mid-level listening where the attention is on the other person (listening for what he or she values and what is important to him or her) to high-level listening where the attention is on the context and impact of what is being said (using my senses and intuition to consider what is not being said).

We use the information we find from careful listening to ask more effective questions. Notice the progression of your questioning. Our questions may move from a simple to a more complex sequence, from describing ("What I hear you saying is . . .") to clarifying ("Here's what I hear you saying. Is that right?) to being curious ("What's motivating you to do this?"). Finally, allow enough silence between finishing a question and getting an answer for a more complete response to bubble up. Classroom teachers are advised to practice the "four-second wait rule" before responding to a question they posed. This gives the student enough time to form a more authentic reply.

These examples of effective questioning and listening have assumed a mutual communication between two or more people. However, this process can also be used as solo practice between your past self and your emerging self. For example:

> ➢ *What feelings came up after I unintentionally broke my diet? (describing)*
>
> ➢ *Do I have a Plan B in place to cover this situation? If not, what would it look like? (clarifying)*
>
> ➢ *What unmet need toppled my intent?*

Effective questions suggest new possibilities. A well-crafted question invites students or clients to consider new perspectives or interpretations of an unexplored reality. Just asking "What's the connection between . . ." expands awareness of a situation which can prompt multiple layers of meaning. Powerful questions can help us suspend judgment so we can get to the good stuff.

The SO WHAT of questioning

Effective questioning of our change process is a bit like the one-shoe-dropping phenomenon. As we wait for the other shoe to drop we are alert to what's coming next. The "So What?" of questioning involves paying closer attention to our own accountability. Not judging your efforts, mind you, but gathering data to allow you to make better decisions so your aliveness can shine. Mahatma Gandhi got to the nut of this matter when he wrote: "As human beings, our greatness lies not so much in being able to remake the world, but in being able to remake ourselves." That said, we will explore two questions, or impediments to realizing our greatness, on the journey to remaking ourselves.

> *How can I undo the priority I give to self-judgment?*

Many people believe that those who are successful are free from self-doubt and insecurities. We've worked with many students and clients whose achievements and reputations are quite admirable, yet their negative self-talk is often utterly brutal. The huge disconnect between their outer success and their inner feelings about themselves causes them to hold back from making changes that would lead to far greater peace of mind. Despite our public success we can't avoid negative self-judgments. It's our protection against rejection or failure. Our internal dialogue chatters away incessantly, "If I judge myself first, then the judgments from others won't sting as much." Yet judgments, of ourselves and of others, send us on a detour from discovering the power to change our lives in positive ways. What's the Rx?

The way out of this predicament is to dive into the mess head first with a curiosity to discern what you can and cannot control. First become aware of the feelings behind the judgment (ex: fear, anxiety, anger, depression, guilt, etc.) and then ask yourself, "Is the narrative behind the feelings 100% true or just a story I am telling myself?" If it is not 100% true, then tap into your inner wisdom and ask, "What is the real truth here?" If you are sincerely open to genuine change, the truth will inadvertently pop into your mind, and it will be much different than the story you've been telling yourself. Following this path makes it easier to let go of resistance and tune in to our deeper passion and move forward with confidence.

We have found two useful ways to foster this sense of self-encouragement. First, disable your self-accuser. Recognize your imperfections and respond by giving yourself unconditional love. In this way you can shut down your emotional triggers and reduce your need to diminish yourself or others. Let silliness replace seriousness in embracing the judgment. For example, replace "I am controlling but I can't live with myself" with "I am polka dot and I can live with myself." Taking away the heaviness of the self-criticism makes it easier to embrace the healing powers of love. Eventually you'll have the courage to say "I am controlling <u>and</u> I am learning to live with myself." Second, vow not to be offended. Know how to sidestep the blame game. After moaning to a friend about an incident where I was treated wrong, a dear friend, remarked, "I've been called everything in the book and I am not offended." Incredulously, I asked, "How?" His reply was so simple, "I ask just one question: 'Is it true?' If it is, I accept it and forgive myself. I don't identify with it. It it's not, then it's not my problem; it's the other guy's stuff?"

> *How can I be happy despite my perceived deficits?*

Developing I/Thou thinking is powerful but don't hold yourself to unrealistic standards and expect a quick transformation of lifelong habits. Although you can never be free of self-judgment you can alter the reception of what they offer and learn from them. Through mindfulness practice and self-inquiry, you can learn to notice when you are tearing yourself down and begin to change your habit of self-criticism. Also, as much as possible, go beyond basic behavior change. Allow your consciousness to expand accordingly. In The Art of Happiness the Dalai Lama points the way to seeing yourself in a new light: "A disciplined mind leads to happiness, and an undisciplined mind leads to suffering. If you want others to be happy, practice compassion. If you want to be happy, practice compassion." So, how can we practice compassion, for ourselves and for others, in our hurried, harried world? We offer four possibilities:

- Meditation

    Happiness is an inside job; practice quieting the mind. Whatever the form (ex: mantra, sitting meditation, tai chi) meditation takes away the distractions of the mind. Happiness is about being, not doing

- Meaning

    Our lives matter. What gives purpose in our life comes from what we value. When we give ourselves, wholeheartedly, to others or a cause we are rewarded with a deep emotional satisfaction.

- Gratitude

    When we acknowledge the good, despite appearances, we become more thankful. Seeing the opportunities hidden in adversity reminds us that we have the gift of choice in how to respond to challenges.

- Generosity

    The more generous we are, the more we get back. For example, Alcoholic Anonymous sponsors are twice as likely to stay sober as non-sponsors. Sharing and giving makes us feel better. When we simply "think" of helping someone, our endorphins increase.

Finally, know that happiness is a byproduct of living well; don't chase after it. Continue developing a disciplined mind by asking essential questions to increase your consciousness and solidify the change you want to see.

The NOW WHAT of questioning

Claiming your light means being aware of your surroundings. That means recognizing your consciousness and how your mind interprets the world. David R. Hawkins, a renowned psychiatrist, researcher and spiritual teacher had a succinct description about how shifting one's consciousness leads to change: "Consciousness advances when it's provided essential information, then activated by intention. This prompts inspiration, humility and surrender which lead to dedication and perseverance." We've tried to follow this formula as we designed this book. We provided essential information through the content of the Key 3, empathy, grit, and growth mindset. We hope the sections on "Listening to Our Inner Quiet" help you develop a stronger intent. We equally hope that the questioning strategies in this chapter prompt inspiration, humility and surrender. Here are a few practical ideas to keep steadfast when dealing with obstacles along the way.

When trying out new life strategies, a good rule of thumb is the "one-step removed" guideline. It's easy to become resistant or distracted when dealing with a problem that has bedeviled you for years. However, given some distance, the same problem which clouds your judgment can look less frightening or confusing. That distance may be of time or person. Here's how "one-step removed" rule works. Think of an embarrassing moment from your recent past that caused you to wince. Perhaps it was some slight that's still tender to the touch. Now think of an embarrassing moment from your distant past, maybe something that happened to you as a child or in middle school or high school. Chances are enough time has passed to heal that mortifying moment from long ago. Ask yourself how you've changed over time to shrug off that uncomfortable encounter. What perceptions have shifted inside that allow you to laugh at something that once gave you pain? What attitude do you now have that calms the spark which provoked you long, long ago? This is your innate wisdom. It's the most updated version of yourself, reminding you that you can survive an embarrassing moment. Now take that wisdom, those new attitudes about yourself, and apply it to the current embarrassment. See, you do have the tools to overcome a potentially negative response. You can break the vicious cycle of victimization.

An alternate pathway to move from victim cycle to virtuous cycle is to think of someone you know who has successfully changed a habit you are now dealing with (like not becoming paralyzed when embarrassed). Go through the same process as you followed when applying wisdom from the past to a present problem. How does this successful someone inspire new behavior? What unexpected attitude does this champion in your life model? The "one-step removed" rule is a way of asking questions of your earlier self or of someone else to help you take the necessary baby steps toward the new territory of sustainable change.

It is important to remember that simply wanting to change a belief is not always enough to make an instant permanent change. Beliefs are programmed deeply into the mind, and you have collected evidence for many years to support them. If you have a setback about an intended goal or new belief, that just means you need to go deeper. Pay attention to the beliefs and agreements inside your mind that support your story of how the world works. Going deeper means accessing your inner guide and knowing the difference between knowledge and wisdom. Knowledge is the information that has been put in your mind by others or by the culture and times in which you live. Wisdom transcends a life limited by an old belief system and opens the heart and mind to celebrate the beauty and wonder inherent in all life.

Trusting your instinct about your innate wisdom creates a personal freedom from limiting beliefs and agreements. To break free of the unconscious programming of these limiting beliefs you must be willing to investigate the memories (and the emotional charge attached to those memories) of the past. Two effective approaches to gain your freedom is through taking a personal inventory and recapitulation. The first step is to take a thorough inventory of every memory in your mind. Make a list, by category, of the people, places and things in your life. Don't be afraid to include traumas to your body or mind and mistakes you have made. Expand that inventory. For example, make a list of "friends," beginning with the most current and going back to the first one. Then break down the relationship of each friend to important time periods of the relationship (ex: she was a colleague for two years; we became friends for 10 years; she moved away and we lost touch). Finally record your body's emotional reaction to any hurt, sadness, anger or other strong emotion. This prepares you for recapitulation. Begin with one item on your inventory. Relax into the memory using conscious breathing to connect to your body's experience of the emotions involved, especially in those places where the energy of the memory is stuck. Feel the truth of the incident or person as you know it. Now shift your mind to a perch above that moment. See the long stretch of time before and after the incident, perhaps several generations of families with all of their pain, fear and confusion. Note also, the limitless boundaries of absolute perfection – the "as is" of life – around this narrow band of memory. From this position, your perceptions naturally shift and you can see a larger truth. You realize this moment in time could not have been any different than it was. There is neither victim nor perpetrator but simply the interconnected stories of repeated rejections which were passed on, consciously or unconsciously, to you. Now back to your breath. On the inhale breath, take in the full measure of that past recollection. On the exhale breath release the constraining energy. Inhale the blocked energy of the memory; exhale the free-flowing energy in this present moment. Continue this conscious breathing until the experience is totally cleared and you are at peace. Repeat this process with every item on your inventory. The cleansing power of the truth releases poison from old emotional wounds. Healing happens as self-love garnered from the boundless abundance surrounding this restricted memory is applied to those wounds. In effect, conscious recapitualization cleanses long-held pain. There is no longer any need to protect that invisible but incessant hurt. This frees up new energy which can be applied to the change you want to see in your life. Finally, after each breath work session, train your brain for new outcomes. Repeat or affirm (again and again) the new belief and assess the evidence that supports the new behavior. Ask yourself with as much honesty as you can handle, am I becoming a more vibrant person?

Listening to Our Inner Quiet

In sports, as in war, there is a defensive game and an offensive game, the former for protecting and the later for scoring. In business, a defensive strategy is designed to reduce the risk of loss, to protect your share of the market in order to keep your customers happy and your profits stable. On the other hand, an offensive competitive strategy pursues changes within an industry, usually with investments in technology and research and development, to be a trend-setter and stay ahead of the competition. Few players, even professional athletes or business leaders, excel at both. This analogy characterizes personal change too. To Claim Your

Light you can choose the carrot approach or the stick approach to fashion your new life. Will I send in the offensive team or the defensive team to gain insight for a fulfilling life? For example, you might employ a defensive strategy towards getting unstuck from negativity by asking yourself how you can stop your personal drama, how you can reduce your loss and address unmet needs? An offensive plan might involve slipping past self-imposed barriers, to break free and score big points to your deeper calling. That means seeing yourself as a trend-setter and following the charge by Henry David Thoreau: "Go confidently in the direction of your dreams! Live the life you've imagined." Here are some questions to live as you put your game plan together:

> *What happened today that made you keep going to satisfy unmet needs?*

> *What did you learn from that? What's your takeaway?*

> *What surprised you or what mistakes did you make that taught you something?*

> *What strategy are you going to try to get back on track?*

Spoiler alert. Living your deepest truth will require you to give up a sizeable chunk of your status quo. Not everything, mind you, just those areas which no longer fit who you are right now, the person you are becoming. Expect pushback, especially from those closest to you. They have grown comfortable with that well-worn older version of yourself.

Your journey toward your dreams might very well challenge their complacency. It is tempting to fall back into the numb-inducing trance that has been the source of your suffering. Change doesn't come with any guarantees. It most certainly doesn't come with a playbook. Expect to encounter danger. And wonder. And surprises galore. So remember the bottom line: you, and only you, are in charge of your life. Let your vision do the talking and be ready to adjust plans along the way. Marcel Proust had it right: "The real voyage of discovery consists not in seeking new landscapes, but in seeing with new eyes."

As he was approaching his own death, Dr. Stuart Farber, a palliative care physician at the University of Washington, reflected on patient care and what he referred to as his thread. "With rare exception, the clinicians who treated me have good hearts, care deeply, but possess little to no knowledge of my thread. My thread is the narrative I use to make sense of my life. It is longitudinal, non-linear and emotional, filled with contradictions, and integrates my life experiences into a coherent whole. It is within the values and meanings of my story that treatment decisions are made. What contributes to meaning and quality is not about living longer but living a life that is consistent with my thread. Without knowing my thread, it is impossible for a clinician to provide respectful care." Indeed. That's the premise of this book, boiled down to 21 words: "What contributes to meaning and quality is not about living longer but living a life that is consistent with my thread." That's the insight that makes for a fulfilling life.

So what's your thread? What's your soul's hunger?

Wayne's story

When I was in my late twenties and early thirties, I had a recurring dream which terrified me. In the dream I was a circus acrobat hanging forty feet above the ground. My job was straightforward: to let go of the handle of one swing, turn to my right 180 degrees and catch an approaching swing in midair. But I wondered, would the approaching swing really be in place when I needed to grab it? What if it came crashing into my body as I completed the turn or, worse yet, be just out of reach? Actually I didn't just wonder . . . I obsessed over the different permutations of disaster that awaited me. It is said that dreams are a reflection of unresolved issues in one's life. True that. It was a period in my life where I needed to master several huge unrelated jobs all at once – a new marriage, new kids and a new job. My career aspirations were the most vexing. How could I possibly carve my own space as a teacher given the high standards set by my mother, an elementary school teacher, and by my father, a college professor? It felt like I was juggling too many balls in the air and I couldn't afford to drop any one of them without dire consequences. No wonder I obsessed over my predicament. My anxiety increased with each passing dream. I turned in midair and froze, blind to my surroundings. The dream seemed to show up when I had too many "must make" deadlines in my life. I needed to release this tension . . . like NOW. I finally hit the wall. Or, more precisely, I hit the floor. One night I was so physically wrapped up in the dream that I fell out of bed! There I sat, dazed, with a goofy grin on my face. "Oh yeah," I thought, "I can look up," This was followed by a rapid-fire awareness, "I can look up or down or to the right or left. I don't have to look just straight ahead." My emotional dam broke. I laughed and laughed until my sides hurt. There was more than one way to look when fear gripped me. I had options. It was like trying on a new pair of eyes. I giggled to myself and got back into bed. Slept like a baby. That dream never returned.

<u>Barb's story</u>

Have you ever felt invisible? Far too often in my personal and professional life I'd have to answer "yes." What makes it even worse is how often it was because of my own choices. Why did I stay in situations that were uncomfortable and left me feeling unfulfilled and empty? In one job I was low woman on the totem pole. My ideas were routinely disregarded and my input was not valued by the team. I voiced my concern with the manager who told me that her view of the workplace was in line with the company's standards. She assumed I understood the culture of the company, even though this code was not verbalized. One day I had an 'Ah ha' moment. I was not there to meet their standards; I was there to be visible. My professional strength of connecting and building relationships with others was not valued in this particular job. I honestly don't even believe they knew what value I could bring to the table. I launched into being visible but that meant a change, I needed to find a place that valued what I valued.

Truth be told, I knew what I wanted. But finding my true path to vulnerability, enlightenment, and depth of self has not been an easy route. I've had so many twists and turns and roadblocks along the way. The most vexing barrier was my need to listen to my truth and respect my own needs instead of only pleasing others. A huge weight was lifted when I left that job precisely because it did not feed my soul. An even larger weight was lifted when I released the negative people and dark energy that drained me of my zest for life. That's my focus now, to keep my zest in the forefront and live a life of opportunity, growth and new possibilities. The journey is now well underway. I will continue to speak my truth as I know it and not knowingly allow myself to become invisible. I am finding my thread.

Recommended Reading

Empathy

Baron-Cohen, Simon, Zero Degrees of Empathy: The New Theory of Human Cruelty and Kindness, Penguin, 2012

Brown, Brene, Rising Strong: The Reckoning, The Rumble, The Revolution, Penguine Random House, 2015

Brown, Brene, The Power of Vulnerability, a TED talk, Jan 3, 2011,
https://www.ted.com/talks/brene_brown_on_vulnerability#t-578185

McLaren, Karla, The Art of Empathy: A Complete Guide to Life's Most Essential Skill,
Sounds True, 2013

Grit

Duckworth, Angela, Grit: The Power of Passion and Perseverance, Scribner, 2016

Hoerr, T., Fostering grit: How do I prepare my students for the real world? ASCD Arias, 2013, p. 52.

Kaplan, Linda Kaplan and Koval, Robin, Grit to Great: How Perseverance, Passion, and Pluck Take You from Ordinary to Extraordinary, Thayer Crown Business; First Edition, 2015

Meadows, Martin, Grit: How to Keep Going When You Want to Give Up, CreateSpace Independent Publishing Platform, 2015

Sharrock, Daisy, Down the Rabbit Hole: An Exploration of Student Grit, CreateSpace Independent Publishing Platform, 2013

Tough, Paul, How Children Succeed: Grit, Curiosity, and the Hidden Power of Character, Houghton Mifflin Harcourt, 2012

Mindset:

Dweck, Carol, Mindset: The New Psychology of Success, Random House, 2006

Four Ways to Develop Growth Mindset, http://growingleaders.com/blog/four-ways-to-develop-a-growth-mindset/

Hogan, Milana L., The Power of Grit and Growth, Chief Learning Officer, August 1, 2014

Motivate Students to Grow Their Mindset, http://www.mindsetworks.com/

Study Smarter ebook, http://inkwellscholars.org/study-smarter/

Consciousness and Calling

Castaneda, Carlos, The Fire from Within, Simon and Schuster, 1984

Eckhart Tolle, Stillness Speaks, New World Library, 2003

Griscom, Chris, The Ageless Body, The Light Institute Press, 1992

Heward, Lyn and Bacon, John U., The Spark: Igniting the Creativity Fire that Lives Within Us All, Cirque du Soleil, Currency Doubleday, 2006

Levoy, Gregg, Callings: Finding and Following an Authentic Life, Three Rivers Press, 1997

McDonnell, Karl, It's All in Your Mind, Chief Learning Officer, August 20, 2014

Richards, M. C., Centering: In Pottery, Poetry, and the Person, University Press of New England, 1989

Biography

Wayne Benenson, Ph.D., has a lot of gypsy energy in him. He has taught in many classrooms, from preschool to grad school, in public and private schools, in 13 different cities. His lifelong quest has been to be available for the teachable moment with whomever and wherever it might show up. He has a keen interest in training school-based peer mediators, coaching for transformational leadership and sensing the feng shui in his office as it extends to the desert view outside the window. In the evening he looks forward to his dog walking him. He can be contacted at wbenenson2700@comcast.net.

Barb Hughson, is the owner and CEO of DurangoLearns, a potpourri of leadership training, nonprofit management courses and continuing education plus practical classes (cooking, spoken Italian, internet graphic design, etc.) led by subject experts from the community. She has used her degrees, a MA and a MS.Ed in Counseling and Education and an Ed.D in Organizational Leadership, to further her passions as a family mediator and children and adolescents therapist. She thoroughly enjoyed her recent incarnation offering faculty training and support at a university in Seattle. She continues working with companies to design and facilitate learning that works for all levels. She can be contacted at CEO@DurangoLearns.com

For further information about our 'Shift' program contact us at wbenenson2700@comcast.net or CEO@DurangoLearns.com.

Go to www.GreatMastersInc.com to join the GreatMasters Tribe and sign up for our great program!

www.ingramcontent.com/pod-product-compliance
Lightning Source LLC
Chambersburg PA
CBHW021130300426
44113CB00006B/366